To find out more:

The writers in this anthology have written for various publications and some have produced books. The reader is invited to use a standard search engine on the Internet to locate the wide range of writing and other activities, some of which will further the reader's knowledge of these very important topics in the world of philosophy, philosophical counseling, Philosophical Midwifery, and spiritual growth.

Philosophical Perspectives
from
Pierre Grimes
and
Opening Mind Writers

An Anthology of Articles and Reviews

originally published in

New Perspectives: A Journal of Conscious Living

compiled by

Allan Hartley

Journal Publisher-Editor

Lulu

Philosophical Perspectives from Pierre Grimes
and Opening Mind Writers

Hartley, Allan, Editor

ISBN 978-0-557-20707-7 (Softbound)

Lulu.com

Assembling materials, initial edit and format by Julie Postel. Text final design/format by Bill Gilbert; cover design by Bill Gilbert, Ronda Gilbert and Nancy Grimes. Proof reading by Nancy Grimes, Ronda Gilbert, and Julie Hoigaard.

Philosophical Perspectives from Pierre Grimes and Opening Mind Writers

Contents

Note: Contributors' last names only are shown in italics enclosed by [ ] in the Table of Contents. The reader is invited to consult the list that follows for more information on the authors. The original author notes from the articles at the time they were published were retained with the arrticle as appropriate.

Anthology Contributors

PIERRE GRIMES, PH.D. wrote many of the articles in this book and was the motivation and inspiration for the contributors of the rest of the articles and reviews to *New Perspectives: A Journal of Conscious Living* of which this book is comprised. Dr.Grimes formed the Noetic Society in 1976, and it was formed into a non-profit corporation in 1978. This gave birth to his philosophical midwifery program. He has taught Classical Philosophy at Golden West College in Huntington Beach, California for 30 years. After more than 40 years, he still moderates the Friday night group meetings. Two of Grimes well-known publications are *Is It All Relative?* and *Philosophical Midwifery: A New Paradigm for Understanding Human Problems with it's Validation.*

JULIE POSTEL (JULIE GRABEL before 2007) managed the Opening Mind Academy online and at a facility in Costa Mesa, California for Dr. Grimes until 2004. Since that time Opening Mind has been a Web Site presence only.

REGINA L. ULIANA, PH.D. is co-author with Pierre Grimes of *Philosophical Midwifery: A New Paradigm for Understanding Human Problems With Its Validation.* She is a clinical and research psychologist and a certified philosophical counselor in Huntington Beach, California.

ROBERT APATOW, PH.D. is the author of *The Spiritual Art of Dialogue: Mastering Communication for Personal Growth, Relationships, and the Workplace.*

MICHAEL COX, PH.D., a former student of Dr. Grimes, also studied Tibetan and Indian Buddhism and Early Christianity at the University of California, Santa Barbara.

CARY COSTNER studied with Dr. Grimes at the Friday Night duscussions intermittently for 28 years. He is a student of Son Buddhism (Korean Zen).

BILL GILBERT, M.A. is a specialist in linguistics/language acquisition. He is Lecturer Emiritus at California State University, Long Beach. He studied Zen Buddhism with Yasutani Roshi, Koryu Roshi, and Maezumi Sensei. He considers himself a Platonist who meditates. Gilbert is the publisher at Hyparxis Press of several of Pierre Grimes' books.

JULIE HOIGAARD, PH.D., is a long time participant at the Friday Night discussions. She is on the staff at University of California, Irvine, teaches psychology at Fullerton Community College. She is a scholar of Son Buddhism (Korean Zen).

JUAN BALBOA is a student of Dr. Grimes and a member of the Opening Mind Academy. He is a scholar in classical Greek.

BARBARA STECKER, M.A. has been a student of philosophy and Philosophical Midwifery with Dr. Grimes for over 30 years. She is a a specialist in second language acquisition and a scholar in classical Greek.

NOBUYA TERAOKA, M.A. teaches mathematics at Golden West College in Huntington Beach, California. He is a scholar in Classical Greek.

BARRY GOLDBERG is President of Imajika Health Products, Inc. and is an independent reviewer.

These writers gave their time and energy and devotion to their disciplines to disseminate information on their various subjects through *New Perspectives: A Journal of Conscious Living*. Their greatly appreciated contributions helped make the *Journal* the comprehensive publication it is.

A. Hartley

Introduction

This is a compilation of articles written by Pierre Grimes, Ph.D. and the members of the Opening Mind Academy and The Noetic Society, Inc. The articles were not submissions, but requests and assignments by me. I get ideas for a story or a publisher sends a book to review, and then I look for the right person to write it. It might appear that New Perspectives was promoting this group and especially Dr. Grimes' work, but actually the articles and reviews just fit the moment or the "news of the day." I will say, though, that their interest in Dr. Grimes' work led many of the writers to try to fit something about him in no matter what the article or review might be about. Why so many articles from one group when I am an independent publication, not promoting any particular philosophy?

Remarkably, with Grimes, the word "no" has pretty much been eliminated from his vocabulary and replaced with "service." That is, the reaction to my asking for a review, an article, a meeting, or something else, is always met with not a no or I'll think about it. It is always, "When do you need it?" This quality of being agreeable to do whatever is needed to be done is refreshing, and one that is not always found among the general population. Julie Postel and others from Pierre's group have this quality as well. So, it stands to reason why there have been so many articles written by these people over the past fifteen years. They are eager to do the work.

I first met Grimes and his group at the Zen Mountain Center near Idyllwild, California in early 1991. They were there meditating and dialoguing. I was doing a three month break from the publication. One of my functions there was as assistant tenso, or cook. I made them breakfast and took a walk with them in the beautiful pine forest. It was several years later when I thought of Dr.Grimes for an article and called him. Various people from his group started writing for New Perspectives sometime later. Grimes began his regular column for us, aptly called "The Philosopher," in 2000.

This book is set up by sections, similar to the magazine. Within each section the article or review is placed in chronological order so that there can be shown a succession of thought or latest topic of interest. Each section is unique except that you find something about Philosophical Midwifery in every section.

Allan Hartley, Editor/Publisher
New Perspectives : A Journal of Conscious Living

Section One: FEATURE ARTICLES

The Art of Delivering Oneself of False Beliefs: Part I, An Introduction to Platonic Philosophy

By Pierre Grimes, Ph.D.

Man is a curious creature. There appears to be nothing he will not try if it offers the slightest chance of overcoming his sense of alienation. He will go to war, use drugs, get married, and even play golf. Even if it has only the slimmest chance of ending his sense of futility, he will gamble on it. The sense of being incomplete has driven many into psychotherapy, it can lead one to search the heavens for some clue to one's destiny, it can awaken a need to meditate in Zen, it can draw one into the priesthood or to coaching little league, and for some it can motivate them to exchange their talent and life's energies to enrich a corporation in return for a vague promise of financial gain and, possibly, retirement. But while nearly anything will be tried, there is one thing that nearly everyone rules out, something that they are sure will never work and that is relying upon one's own reason to lead to resolvement of their conflicts and their dissatisfaction with life. For, life is lived through the mind, conflicts are only resolved through the mind, and through that solution the unity of life and the mind is recognized. The realization of the profound unity of our existence is the foundation for a deeper understanding of the mystery of our existence. The way to that realization and understanding is the ancient path of philosophy.

However, the idea of philosophy most people are acquainted with is derived from a European tradition that is hostile, or indifferent, to spiritual goals and metaphysics. Philosophy in the European tradition is an attempt to discover a place for knowledge in history, language, science, and even common sense but not in the quest to know thyself. Those that have turned to the most profound of Eastern philosophies have discovered in their very quest for the Self that reason and intellect do not play a primary role there either. In our own educational institutions the idea of pursuing a philosophy that is centered around the quest for wisdom would be regarded by most as not only unscientific but irrelevant if not heretical to the direction of contemporary thought and philosophy. It has been argued by some that in our society there is a pervasive skepticism and distrust of reason; clearly, it is not that reason has failed, for the truth is that we have ignored our past, not rejected it; our culture has not kept alive the profound traditions of our past. Thus, the claim that philosophy can reach meaning and can explain the dynamics of mind is something most people would find hard to understand.

The ancient Greeks, in contrast with European tradition, had cultivated a philosophy and traditions that centered around the quest for wisdom that had granted them profound spiritual goals. An adaptation of this philosophy has disclosed that we are in the grip of a strange kind of problem, one that we hadn't suspected we have. It has been demonstrated that any false belief about oneself and the nature of reality has sufficient force to block one from the attainment of one's highest aspirations and most meaningful goals. A further difficulty: They are virtually invisible to the believer. Since they are not identified by the believer as something they themselves believe, they cannot recall it nor reflect upon it. Curiously then, these false beliefs are accepted as intuitively certain yet are not recognized as being believed by the believer. Clearly, this is the worst of ignorance, to believe one is intelligent and good enough without realizing the depth of our ignorance and just how far we have slipped from realizing our ideals; while the need for understanding oneself and reality is desperate, we remain indifferent to our plight.

It might be asked: If we are ignorant, how can philosophy offer an approach to the problem of ignorance? The practice of philosophy starts with ignorance, or not knowing, and charts a journey through the intellectual domain to right opinion, to understanding and to knowledge or wisdom; it moves as if by a flight of stairs, until one reaches that perfect learning called wisdom. Being ignorant is the state of mind when one's false beliefs about oneself and reality block one's own development. It has been demonstrated that since these false beliefs are irreconcilable with one's highest goals and aspirations, they are the inevitable cause of our failures and disillusionment with our lives. When you learn the right opinion you have the right answer without understanding the reasons why it is a right opinion. The way to discover these reasons is, of course, the exercise of reason. Again, someone may ask what kind of reasoning and practice is this that can eliminate those beliefs that you never knew you believed.

Well, reason is what it is, whenever the conditions allow it to be, then it naturally emerges. The way reason functions in philosophy is no different than the way it functions in the sciences. Consider, do we not say that reason allows us to discover the causes of the patterns we observe? The patterns can be in our behavior, in our dreams, or into the subatomic world of quarks and superstrings. When we search into the causes of the patterns discovered in the heavens, it is called cosmology; when it is into the causes of our believing false beliefs, into the processes of reaching understanding, and into the nature of mind, it is called philosophy. If what is found to lie at the root of man's irrational behavior are false beliefs, then the discipline that identifies and resolves these false beliefs through the exercise of understanding is what should be cultivated. The struggle to reach understanding develops the understanding; the struggle to get out of problems is the cultivation of understanding.

Surely now if this is true, there should be a way to lead another to an exploration of their particular problem. There should be a way to find the false beliefs that underlie each problem. Each problem has its own unique roots, but since the general form of all problems is much the same, then a set of questions should be designed to serve this need. Indeed, a set of questions has been developed to meet this very need. These questions have introduced people into self-reflection and many people to the art of delivering oneself of false beliefs. They were designed to be part of a program to teach this art. It was called "A Guide For Your Reflections: A Journey into Philosophical Midwifery" and we have adapted them for your reflections. These questions will bring to the surface the nature of a person's problem, either your own problem or someone you might care to share them with. It does take some skill to fully understand the material brought up by the questions, but when they are reflected upon again and again, the mind is brought to see distinctions and connections in the material and that network of connections found in the material becomes the basis of a new understanding of oneself and reality. It is like the polishing of a gem—it can gain luster by repeated polishing. Let us start, then, with the signs of a problem in PART II in the next issue of New Perspectives.

New Perspectives: July, 1994, pp. 26-28.

The Art of Delivering Oneself of False Beliefs: Part II, The Signs of a Problem

By Pierre Grimes, Ph.D.

The art that assists men in bringing to birth their ideas was called Philosophical Midwifery by Socrates. I have adapted this Socratic art and applied it to a new member in the class of belief that we call pathologos. And you by practicing this method are becoming philosophical yourself. Philosophy does go beyond this level of belief and passes into the realm of understanding and knowledge, but a discussion on that aspect of this ancient art of Philosophical Midwifery would require another article. Those who can pass through these stages can be called philosophical midwives, and they become members of a new profession whose goal is to demonstrate that reason and understanding can free men from their own oppressive ignorance. Those who can participate in this activity become a part of a profound tradition that was interrupted when Emperor Justinian prohibited the teaching of philosophy and closed Plato's Academy in 529 A.D.

Man's fate depends upon only one thing. It is something he is aware of yet often seeks to escape, and in this flight he turns away from his destiny. What we need to face is our everyday problems because in their solution lies clues for the resolving of our fate. But what is a problem? When we try to avoid one we know we create greater turmoil for ourselves. Surely since there are different kinds of problems, just what kind of problem are we referring to? Some are far more serious than others.

To grasp the nature of the kind of problem we are describing, it is necessary to distinguish between a difficulty one may have and what we shall call a problem. Let us then give the name *pathologos* to the kind of problem we shall discuss. As the name suggests, pathologos means a 'sick idea' and refers to a special kind of problem. Now, the signs of having a pathologos, or problem, are very simple to state. If in examining the list that follows you can identify any of these signs with your own present condition, then you can say you have a pathologos.

Signs of a Problem

- Not striving for one's most personally meaningful goals.
- Failing to achieve one's goals with excellence.
- Setting secondary goals as primary.
- Making practical issues the main or significant goals.
- Letting opportunities go by, sabotaging opportunities for success.
- Not preparing adequately for goals:
  - Losing concentration and energy,
  - Being unable to resist distraction,
  - Blaming others, excuses.
- Being unable to maintain the goal.
- Functioning ideally in crises, but experiencing stress and anxiety before and after such events.

Please notice that what we are defining as a problem is much different than what most people call a problem. It is a special kind of problem. The roots of this kind of problem are learned and are based upon accepting a false belief about oneself and reality; and it is something you don't even know you believe. It is because of these differences that we give it a new name and call it the pathologos, which means sick idea. Therefore, as the name indicates, the kind of problem we are discussing is not the same as experiencing difficulties in life, because it is natural to experience some difficulty while in pursuit of one's goals. Encountering difficulties, on the other hand, is different than dealing with the pathologos because one can learn to solve difficulties or discover ways to avoid them and this is what is not possible with the pathologos.

We can learn from our mistakes in the one, but not with the other. Thus, there are essential differences between experiencing difficulties and the pathologos.

Now, since you know there are few things more important than reflecting on your own life, you might want to arrange your time so you can devote sufficient time and attention to this important task. Secondly, after you write down your answers in your journal, study them, review them, and add to them as you recall new material and insights. So then, let us explore a troublesome problem you are having.

I. State the nature of your problem

1. The first step is to state as clearly as you can the nature of your problem. What reasons do you give yourself for not achieving your highest goals?
2. As you consider these goals and why you have not achieved them, could you explain the effect this failure has had on your life?
3. Again, what is it like when you anticipate facing these problems in your daily life?

II. Describe the scenes in the present and the recent past

Now take this present difficulty you are having, and as you review it, see if you can determine when it began. Consider the stages it went through, and see if you can identify just where in those stages you felt most "down," depressed, or in some negative state. In the same way, identify the stage(s) where you experienced a "high" and when it was most intense.

1. Further, choose two or three times in the recent past, say within the last few days or weeks, when you felt "down," or were not yourself, and after recollecting these events, please write them down.
2. Carefully compare and contrast this description with the "high" and "down" states you described in 1 above. Examine the sequences of the events for their similarities and differences.
3. Can you explain why these intense "highs" and "downs" occur as they do? Does the presence of these states of mind signal your problem? Is that what it means to have a problem—to face the consequences of these states of mind?

III. Recall early incidents

Now, keep your mind on the description you just gave of these states of mind and reflect on the role they have played in your life.

1. Recall early incidents in your life when you experienced these states of mind most intensely. Please make notes on your reflections. How old were you then? Who was present? Describe the states of mind of those present.
2. What was said at that time? Try to recall the words as precisely as you can. Can you recall the times when you experienced these same words and expressions as thoughts? What effect do those thoughts have upon you? If those thoughts occur when you are trying to achieve a goal—one that is personally significant to you—do these thoughts help or hinder your chance of success?

Note: It sometimes happens that the incident that you recall may not be one in which you experienced the same state of mind as in your present situation; and that is because you may either have experienced someone other than yourself in that particular feeling state, or you may find it difficult or nearly impossible to recall a particular emotional state in your past. If so, consider if it might be that you often experience that state of mind, or have experienced it for a long period of time; and if this is the case, just choose some time when that state of mind was more intense than at other times. In either case, write down what comes to your mind and continue with your reflections.

IV. Reflect on that early scene

Now it is necessary to reconstruct that early scene in as much detail as possible. Picture that scene again as if you were watching it being rerun or, reenacted. Describe that scene. What impact did it have on you? What effect did it have on the others?

1. *After:* What did you do after the most intense part of the drama? Did you say anything? Where did you go? Again, what did those around you do after they saw this scene occur?
2. *Before:* In the same way, describe what happened before that intense scene that you just described. Go back into your recollections to recall all that you can that preceded that scene, asking yourself what you and those around you were doing and what was said.
3. *Beginning:* Now, please describe the state of mind you were in as this scene began. *Note: Now, if you have not recalled a scene when you were living with your parents, or when you were a child, go through these same questions, only this time go back to the time when you were younger and living in your parents' home.*

V. Continue Reflecting

It is essential that you continue reflecting and exploring those scenes until you can recall nothing new. Try these questions to help your recollections:

Was there a special discipline scene? A particular degree of punishment? Was there a fight? Was there an intense argument? A peak of yelling? Or was there no violence, no injury?

1. How was the "making up" scene enacted? Where? What room? Who was there? What was said? What did they and you do?
2. How did you know when it was over? How did you know when you could "forget it?" How was peace or a truce established?

VI. Chart the event, show the cycle

Chart the event, or picture it in terms of a time sequence. See if you can put it into a circle; include all the states, because a problem plays itself out periodically as a cycle or circle. You can use this chart later as a personal mandala.

VII. Reflect further

You must reflect further on what you have done. Consider these questions:

1. How intense were these scenes? How alert and aware were you, and what of the others who were in these scenes?
2. Even though it may have been negative, how much concern was shown you? How much attention was focused on you? Were they showing what mattered most to them? How intimate was it?
3. If the worst thing is to be merely tolerated, because we must know how others feel towards us, then how important is this display of emotion and feeling?
4. When there is no crisis, how do they appear? As real, as powerful, as knowing and as sincere as during the crisis? Did they or you ever show that much feeling at other times? Then can you see why it is at such times that feelings are shown and displayed?
5. Was this event teaching you something? Was it being learned even though you may have preferred some other lesson?
6. Was the lesson you were *learning* at that time connected with your being accepted and being understood? Is this the time they can show you they care? Does this become the moment when they demonstrate they care?
7. Do you see this is one way of showing feelings of concern, even of love, because it is difficult to see the genuine marks of love, and so we are driven to communicate it in ways which we were shown love and concern in our own youth?

8. Compare the states of mind when the scene began and during the last episode in that scene. Did you move better to worse? Does your present state of mind reflect this last episode?
9. How frequently did such scenes occur? Looking back, could you say you could have or should have been able to predict their occurrences? Why?

VIII. Reflect back on the statement of your problem

Reflect on the first stage, the statement you made of your problem, and consider whether that statement fits the past scene and if it is a better way to understand the past than the present. Could a problem statement made in the present actually be a conclusion or a lesson of something learned from a past scene? Why?

IX. Reflect and puzzle out the meaning

Now that you have written down all that you have seen, it is time to reflect upon it, and puzzle out its meaning. If you see the structure or pattern of your problem repeating itself through your life and can see how it is passed down to each generation, then you have come to acknowledge that it is this that is the cause of your confusion, despair, and suffering. Well, if this is so, then can you get out of it? Yes. If it is a problem it can be solved. Study it carefully. Look for more details, find connections, and avoid generalities. Watch yourself when you experience similar states of mind and look for similarities with your past. Study yourself and let your present be a mirror through which to emerge from your past.

Notice another thing. You may see that you are presently in a role that actually was that of another member of your family, perhaps your father's or mother's; that's right, for a problem continues to be played out even when we no longer play the child role.

A problem is *learned*; we learn from others how to play it; it will survive our death. Just as you learned from your parents, so you will pass it on to those intimate with you, unless, of course, you decide to end it now by seeing it fully and consciously.

When you feel curious about whether you have really understood a problem or not, you may find this question of value: What was happening that made the problem surface? What was going on that made its appearance necessary? Clearly, if you don't see that, then it is likely you will return to the problem again because there is still some part obscure to you. If this is so, study yourself further, look more closely, talk about it, and you will come to see what has escaped your attention. Thus the art of delivering oneself of false beliefs must include testing the truth of one's understanding by facing once more those problems in your everyday experience and discovering whether or not you can now achieve your ideal goals. If you do not succeed with excellence, return again for further analysis and reflection.

Accepting the challenge to answer these questions is the doorway into philosophy, not European, nor Eastern, but Platonic philosophy. In the process of resolving problems the most important ideas in philosophy are placed in review: justice, courage, love, understanding, beliefs, and knowing. When we concluded as we did in the early scenes, we accepted the image and shadow of those ideas as real and those shadows became the pathologos. From these early scenes we reached conclusions that became believable because we believed those who appeared believable. They appeared sincere, noble, knowing, and caring so that we in turn would accept their message. We traded the genuine and real for the false and delusionary and so we passed into the world of false beliefs. When we are in the grip of the pathologos we judge everything through it; in judging through it we are locked into reducing everything to the beliefs of the pathologos, and in that reduction we experience an alienation from those most important to us and a sense of futility because we cannot achieve our most cherished dreams and ideals. A pathologos blocks us from fulfilling our destiny and makes us live a life without reflection. Our fate becomes a shadow of the real, but we can recover our direction and become a part of nobler vision that is the true flower of man's destiny.

Dr. Grimes formed The Noetic Society in 1978 which gave birth to his Philosophical Midwifery program.

New Perspectives: Nov./Dec. 1994 pp. 10-13

The Greening of Oakland

A discussion with Jerry Brown on the Oakland Green Plan

By Robert Apatow, Ph.D.

As a self-proclaimed "recovering politician," Jerry Brown today offers penetrating insights into the reality of contemporary politics. Until recently on weekdays at 4 p.m. PST on the Pacifica radio network, the former California Governor could be heard on his show, "We The People," offering political commentary and interviewing leading progressive thinkers.

Brown unfolds what he calls the interconnected web of political corruption that blocks any genuine social or environmental progress from occurring. According to Brown, "The world works for a number of people. More people are living longer. There's more money, there's politicians getting elected. I think people just have to rise up and start doing stuff where they are; and when crises occur, if there's enough leadership, we'll move in the right direction."

In the face of such a complex and powerful system that unites money, politics, business, and the media, Brown is now directing his energies according to the idea "Think Globally, Act Locally." After his defeat in the 1992 presidential campaign, Brown began We The People, a nonprofit organization working toward social and environmental justice. Headquartered in Oakland, the organization sponsored his radio show, tai chi, meditation, lectures, gardening programs, and a School of Sustainability that teaches people how to better their lives and community.

The primary goal of We The People is currently a green plan for the city of Oakland. In an interview for this article Jerry Brown discussed this project. "The concept of a green plan is relatively new. It involves some very long-range thinking that integrates a number of different aspects that shape a region, a city, or even a nation. The green plan idea for Oakland is the linking together of equity, ecology, and aesthetics to pull together people in such a way that they understand the limits and possibilities of living in the 21st century. It draws on former economic development plans, it draws on environmental studies in various fields, and it has a very strong component of popular participation. What we're doing is laying out a framework and then using that framework to engage in a series of conversations throughout the city, enabling people themselves in their neighborhoods to shape the vision of their physical surroundings and how they want to live."

The central idea behind a green plan is the concept of sustainability. According to the United Nations, a sustainable society meets the need of the present population without sacrificing the ability of future generations to meet their own needs. There are currently a number of national and international organizations helping people all over the world generate green plans to help cities and nations strive towards the ideal of a sustainable way of life.

Whereas political planning is often aimed towards short-term ideological or economical ends, a green plan is able to outline long-range goals and principles that a community can work toward. The green plan for San Francisco, for example, (which can be accessed on the Internet) is broken down into the major categories that constitute civic needs: health, transportation, social justice, space, etc. In each area there is an evaluation of the current state, the major concerns, and a plan that outlines goals and steps towards the accomplishment of those goals.

"Currently there are initial outlines of the Oakland green plan," but Brown says that these things are not the kinds of things that are completed and walked away from. "It's a working project. Because our whole thrust in this society is one of throw away, waste and sprawl, turning that around and getting people to understand what it is that is required is not something you can do overnight. It's a process more than a physical plan. Although it has structure in terms of its outline and traditional planning, it's an invitation to conceive of the world in terms of ecological insights and to link those with the goals we normally have for cities, that is, equity and economic well-being."

In the face of economic and political realities, a green plan may seem overly idealistic. For example, if you examine the San Francisco green plan, you will notice that much of the change that will occur in our cities depends on a major shift in the priorities of government. Real change will occur when tax incentives and regulations are established in support of sustainable practices, rather than short-term economic ones. Tax incentives have to be made for recycling and businesses using environmentally friendly processes and materials. Disincentives and regulations have to be aimed at the unsustainable practices.

When leaders move in this direction, the potential benefit is enormous. In fact, the tax breaks that Jerry Brown legislated as governor established the solar-power industry. Today, the solar industry generates jobs, money, and the vital technology needed to achieve a sustainable future. Most industries today, however, are not run in a sustainable manner, and most government leaders are unaware of the environmental principles of sustainability present in green plans.

"I was talking to some people (in Oakland) about the fact that there are 3.7 million miles driven every day and this particular plan's idea of reducing miles driven, and this person said this thought had never been raised. These thoughts may be in the minds of certain environmental writers but they're not in the down-to-earth development concepts—conversations that are going on in the cities of this country."

A green plan is a way to educate these leaders. It is a document that presents a comprehensive analysis of the status of a city or nation in respect to its environmental goals. Green plans establish a dialogue between leading thinkers in every aspect of civic planning and bring out the progressive ideas and concepts that are needed to achieve a sustainable future. They present an ideal and a way of thinking that is an alternative to the current short-term, financially motivated planning that rules political thinking.

And how are civic leaders responding? "I'd say it's too early. The notion of the environment, except when it's toxic waste in your backyard or some visible soot, is something that doesn't grab people in an immediate way unless they see the connection to disease."

So how does Brown see that change coming about? "Only through people and consciousness. As people understand and make it their own and come up with their own insights on how to live within the rules of ecology and the rules of nature, then sustainability becomes an actual operating design."

And yet people seem to put up with the smog and growing ugliness and danger of our industrial economy. "People adjust," Brown says. "People live in slums, they live in smog. We're in a very economic age. Money makes a big difference. It is capitalism. Capital talks. Some of these more long-term values are not obvious to people."

According to a meeting of world leaders in Rio a few years ago, the shift away from consumerism and a change in current values is one of the primary changes that needs to be addressed. When asked how he sees this issue, Brown says, "The values that we're really talking about are really common sense values: frugality and friendship, and being more respectful of the land on which you live. These are ancient truths that people have lived by until relatively recent times. What I'm calling for is the recapturing of common sense and traditional wisdom and I think the people are way ahead of the politicians on that score, and it's real common sense. You ask people do you want to have a healthy environment, and 80 percent of the people say yes. It is only the power of short-term financial advantage that keeps pushing against what people know is the right way to do things."

Brown often warned on his radio show of the danger of the globalization of power. And yet in the coming era of environmental challenges that we will certainly face this writer wonders whether such unified power may be necessary to effect the major changes that will be required for the health of the planet.

"Obviously global weather can only be affected by global decision making. On the other hand, at the bedrock of change is the way people live and the way our lives are organized and that is an individual, local, here-and-now kind of challenge. In terms of the big picture, nations are selling arms and fostering unsustainable and dangerous ways of living and acting, and that has to be changed so that the United Nations and other forums can be places where the change can be made. But I believe the energy for this mode of power is going to have to come from individuals, charismatic leadership, grass-roots activism. Native peoples (worldwide) are still being destroyed; their habitat is being ripped apart by oil companies with the express approval of the United States government, and German and Japanese, and all these other so-called civilized people, and that's got to be turned around. However, the institution of nation states can certainly be enlisted in the cause of justice and sustainability. Tragically, this doesn't happen often enough."

Although leading scientists warn of the imminent danger facing our environment and lives, in many respects the level of environmental problems has not reached the point where people are ready to demand drastic change. Brown hopes that these changes can take place before such an environmental catastrophe does occur.

The problem is that "we don't know where we are. People in Monsserat didn't know until the volcano started erupting, so there is a volcano of environmental disruption that is being fed by the very being of modern economic activity and it is very hard to get people to awaken to that. [But change] is happening. There was a global summit. There is a meeting in Kyoto about climate. These things are happening. Now does that mean somebody in Orange county is thinking about the new toll road that they're making, or what this is doing to endangered species, or [that they're] designing new villages in Orange County so that they can walk to work without driving? [Change is occurring] very, very mildly, but its happening, so the news is both good and bad."

Brown articulates clearly the nature of the problems and crises that face our cities, nations, and our planet. But with crisis there is also the remarkable potential for change and growth. Brown's work attests to that. If we are going to survive and flourish in the next century, we must elicit the help of the progressive thinkers in every field that offers benefit and guidance in human life, from farming, engineering, politics, civic design, to spiritual growth.

Robert Apatow has studied environmental issues for many years. He has a doctorate in philosophy and is the author of *"The Spiritual Art of Dialogue: Mastering Communication for Relationships, Personal Growth and the Workplace."* Information provided in this article was obtained from Apatow's interview with Jerry Brown, Brown's radio show, and web site.

New Perspectives: Winter 1997-98, pp. 12-14

The Symmetry: Excerpts from the Play

By Pierre Grimes, Ph.D.

At a conference sponsored by the Church of Religious Science, Pierre Grimes met a young woman who had a headache. The severity of her headache kept her awake the preceding night. On the spot, in front of everyone in attendance, he took this woman through a dialogue which he identified as Socratic midwifery. The idea of midwifery is a way of dialoguing with another person to assist them in giving birth to the ideas that puzzle and block them. They were able to confront false beliefs about her relationship with her mother and relieve the constant headaches at the source.

This inspired Pierre to write a dialogue or Platonic play based on this spontaneous experience. The result is "The Symmetry" given at the Holmes Institute for the Church of Religious Science in Santa Barbara September 6, 1999 for the first time. The following are the speeches by Sophron addressed to the various characters and those people in attendance at the conference. He talks of dreams, rationalism, mysticism, symmetry, and the introduction to a lengthy dialogue between Sophron and Julie where the audience witnesses the practice of Philosophical Midwifery played out.

Dreams

I found each of these talks revealed much about what concerns you. It gave me the opportunity to enter into the dilemma that you experience. It may not appear that what I will say about dreams may meet your profound needs but I do think that it will do so because it opens a path that is no stranger to the divine.

I speak as someone who has spent much time studying the world of dreams; they are man's gift from the divine. The world of dreams is the doorway into an intellectual and more rational world, because it can introduce you to a profound way of learning about yourself that is providential. If I can make this clear it should provide you with a way to understand that there is a symmetry between the intelligible world and our everyday way of existing, which is to say between the spiritual realm and the mundane.

What is illuminated through dreams is what is most appropriate to one's circumstances, so that each dreamer receives a particular good according to his or her immediate needs. To extend to all a good that is uniquely appropriate to each is to bestow on each what is providential to them. Surely, in filling intelligent beings with their goodness, the master of our dreams bestows upon all things that are capable of receiving it their particular good. It is for this reason that we can say that the dream master exercises providence towards all intelligent beings; for what she communicates is a good most appropriate to the dreamer's needs.

It is through the dream world that there is a return to one's source, to that place where reflections drawn from one's past and present are brought together for our benefit. Dreams are a profound source of guidance and in contemplating them they become our natural object of contemplation.

All intelligent beings are guided by this guiding knowledge. It is this knowledge that always benefits and it is in fact the source of all knowledge. The only real and genuine knowledge is based upon and derived from dreams, since skills and crafts merely utilize the higher forms of knowledge for particular purposes. For it is through the reflection upon dreams that mankind has learned to use metaphors, personifications, similes, symbols, analogies, and allegories.

The structure of the dream presents images metaphorically, and the states of mind experienced in the dream are treated as similes, which brings an understanding of the mystery of the dream content. Clearly these are the tools necessary to express the deepest desires of man, and in communicating what he has learned through these tools he becomes and participates in the rational. The more we can enter into an understanding of this dream world the more we can consciously join in our own development and nurture and become partners in our own evolution, and in this way we learn how the dream master communicates. Strangely enough, when we learn to understand this kind of communication we discover that there is no need to interpret dreams, for in finding our own book of meaning we gain confidence in our own intellectual ability and appreciate the need for understanding ourselves in our own terms.

Pathologos

The dream master's ability to select from each dreamer's own past what has been ignored, and for the most part forgotten, is a sign that the dream master has a profound understanding of each individual's life and destiny. The states of mind presented through the dream, bear a likeness to a past scene in which one unknowingly concluded falsely about oneself and the reality confronting them. Being unaware that one carries these false conclusions into one's understanding of the present, one is trapped to repeat the past as if it were the present. The repetition of mistakes means that one has imposed upon the present a past pattern whose urgency obscures its irrational character. This unknowing superimposed upon the present a past pattern whose urgency obscures its irrational character. This unknowing superimposition of past beliefs upon the uniqueness of the present is the source of pathologos problems. It is by discovering how the dream relates to the everyday experiences of life that one is awakened to the dream's analogical structure. And to unfold the mystery of the dream's content analogically is to recognize a dream as an allegory for the soul's development into its own good.

As long as the particular language of the dreamer expresses false beliefs about the self, which we call a pathologos, there is always a block to the understanding. Once we reach an understanding of how the pathologos fetters and locks the soul's progress there is a natural growth into the logos itself, for the images and relationships expressed in the dream mirror the soul's unknowing loyalty to one's false beliefs.

Dream Master's Art

The dream master's ability to diagnose and chart each dreamer's voyage shows the dream master's profound art of navigation and a knowledge of each of our storm-like struggles as we seek to become masters of our fate. Through each of our voyages we learn to become masters of ourselves and to navigate our uncertain seas. The mastery we gain here is for another journey, one that brings us along a sacred way that all our earlier hardships have prepared us for, one that brings us to the source and goal of all.

Thus, since an application of a knowledge for the benefit of the subject is called a profession or an art, we can conclude that the dream master possesses the highest art, for the benefit of all who are capable of receiving and sharing in it.

The dream master then is our teacher and guide on a road that carries those who know through their life's journey. In the dawning realization that we are, indeed, a part of a caring universe we put aside the need for an unknowing belief in these things, and by that transition from belief to understanding we participate in a more wondrous caring universe. Now you can see why we say the dream master possesses an art, but it would be unfair to say all this without going on to say the rest. Yet, to share this nobler part with you I do not think I shall be able to sing worthily. Still it must be said if truth is to be our guide. You see, this role of midwifery in personal problems, and even providing us with prophetic dreams and insights, is only a small part of the dream master's art. It is the higher and the more profound we must speak of next.

To begin with, let me say that I am not a stranger to what I shall share with you. Indeed, I have been fortunate to be able to say that I have verified within myself, through my own dream experience, all that I say. First, then, the direct participation into that intelligible realm is of such a wondrous nature that once experienced all else is like a shadow compared with it. It has been said that we are very fortunate that we do not see this awe-inspiring numinous presence with the human eye; for if we had, it would arouse in us a truly terrible love. The intelligible is Beauty; it is not different from mind. What is that but mind knowing itself in a divine radiance whose luminosity cannot be other than the most brilliant light of Being? It is because even this, the profoundest of all experiences, is open to us through dreams that the dream master can be said to have a divine source. For that which bestows upon us this wonder of wonders must itself be held in a higher honor than the gift bestowed. I wish to thank you for the opportunity to reflect with you and for your attentive listening.

Interpretation

You are bringing up the fundamental problem of our age: the nature and use of interpretation within systems. It is a curious problem that needs our attention. In what condition must the original work be if it needs to be interpreted? The degree to which a work needs to be interpreted, to that very degree the work itself is weak and needs something outside itself to support it. For surely if it needs to be added to or if parts should be ignored, then in modifying the work in this way the interpreter transforms the work to represent another viewpoint that was not contained in the original work. For to interpret means to add, subtract, or modify some material so that it expresses the interpreter's own viewpoint, and in going beyond the work the interpreter needs to appear both as sincere and as possessing more insight and knowledge than what was formerly believed true.

The believer must have been convinced that the interpreter knows what should have been seen before the interpretation, or there would be no reason to believe the interpretation. Thus, the act of believing is at the same time the moment of sacrificing one's own understanding. It is this forfeiting of one's own understanding that allows an authority to be placed over oneself, and when that authority's interpretation cannot be questioned, tyranny is born. This process is part of the art of rhetoric and is akin to the creating of illusion, or magic. It is certainly important to understand this issue. I would like to offer a demonstration workshop based upon this game of interpretation in order to show the dynamics for inculcating belief, but for now we must return to the other issues that you raised.

I will gladly explore this difficulty that your friend has reported, but as for its outcome, neither I nor you can predict it. Is there something to pain, to a sleepless night, or being late, and such things? Is there a moment without meaning? Is it at all possible that there are no chance elements in our existence? Are there events without meaning, such as accidents? Is meaning the symmetry between everyday events and the intelligible? And if there is, can we discover it? Very nice questions.

Reason

Perhaps it is as you say, but try another direction. Why not consider the obvious? Man is not rational, but he can become rational, and that is only if he learns how to be rational. It is possible to bring rationality into man's various activities, but only if we have discovered how to introduce it into our own activity. The forces against the introduction of reason are formidable, but it is at least in principle possible to do so if we can discover and use rational models.

The culture we have inherited from Europe has been convinced that man is irrational, driven by instinctual urges; and whatever rationality man does possess is regarded as only a veneer, a mask that covers his irrational nature. Reason is believed to be much like a computer, something that processes logical structures, but is impotent and incapable of nurturing man.

Take a look at the various forms of psychotherapy. They all assume that purely rational procedures are ineffective in helping man reach a state of being that is both rational and free of conflict. Our culture is willing to try anything if it offers even a slim chance of being able to change man for the better, and that includes punishment, drugs, starvation, electric shock treatments, prefrontal lobotomy, and inculcating beliefs. The only thing it can't imagine might be beneficial is the cultivation of reason. This is so simply because they don't know what it is.

Platonic Philosophy

Man can become rational. The fullest flowering of the mind can be nurtured and developed through a Platonic vision of philosophy. Indeed, even a single ray of its brilliance is enough to awaken thinkers. It may not be known as it should, but Augustine and Thomas Aquinas were both indebted to Platonic thinkers and without them they could not have developed their systems. Without those deep and nourishing roots they are left with empty rituals and a religious rhetoric that has lost its meaning.

Actually, if we are to speak accurately we should say that there is no Platonic philosophy or tradition, because it is really a rational vision that leads to the unfoldment of mind that culminates in a vision of the nature of reality. If anyone accepts that it is possible to participate in this realm, and from such experience can infer the ideas and categories necessary to build a coherent system, then they are pursuing a rational, reflective philosophy that some can call Platonic. Others would say they are merely using their own mind.

New Perspectives: Autumn 1999, pp. 58-60

Philosophical Counseling and Philosophical Midwifery versus Psychotherapy

Philosophical Midwifery is especially explained by one of its advocates.

By Regina L. Uliana, Ph.D.

There has been a movement in the field of psychology to extend its boundaries into the biomedical field and bring under its domain the prescription of psychiatric medications; in like fashion there has been a movement among philosophers to enter the marketplace and to extend their boundaries into human problem solving. Different from each of these is a movement that seeks to reintroduce a metaphysical turn of mind as a viable form of human understanding, study and spiritual practice. These systems each bring along their own controversy for they are competing with the prevailing tides and winds of what is taught and assumed to be true.

In part, such movements are economically driven. But of greater significance are their assumptions about the nature of humankind, which in turn influence the way they treat humankind's ailments and dilemmas.

For example, from the beginning of the 20th century to the present, modern psychology has been dominated by those who assume that human experiences can be understood in terms of biochemical and physiological processes. Accordingly, research and treatment guided by these empirically-based assumptions and influenced by the medical model seek to understand psychological problems and disorders in terms of chemical imbalances, maladaptive behaviors and/or pathological environments. As a consequence the patient becomes the passive recipient of interpretations, advice, medications and behavioral programs.

When Albert Ellis, author of Rational-Emotive Psychotherapy (RET), introduced the role of cognitions as a major factor in psychological problems, it appeared that psychotherapy was opening the door to study the mind from a non-empirical position (not as a brain with neurons and synapses) where ideas, beliefs, and patterns of thinking could be explored by purely rational procedures. But RET and other cognitive psychotherapies assume that the cognitions, called irrational beliefs, can be better studied and treated by empirical-behavioral learning models. So what appeared to be a new direction in psychology was actually a new dress on an old model. Like their predecessors, these new cognitive-behavioral theories assume that the causes of a person's irrational thinking have their sources in non-rational factors such as the libido, poor modeling, pathogenic environments, etc. Consequently, treatment by purely rational methods would be seen as futile. They left then untended those areas that hypothesize a purely rational approach. One such contender for this open space has been the relatively new philosophical counseling movement that began in the 1980s. In general this new movement assumes that everyone has a philosophy of life. These personal world views may not be evident, but when people try to solve their personal dilemmas or cope with the challenges that face them, they often fall back on their particular world views. Sometimes one's world views are inadequate and limit one's way of handling life's difficulties and challenges. To address these apparent inadequacies, there are some philosophers staking claims that they can expand the horizons of one's "world view," and thus one's growth and development, by using philosophical methods of reasoning as an alternative to or in conjunction with medications or prescribed behavioral programs to meet various life challenges. They offer the promise that some of the "abstract ideas" that philosophers debate about can be useful on a personal level.

Some philosophical counselors also believe modern psychotherapies have been ineffective in handling many of the more complex questions that many people have, such as: What is the meaning of life and death? What is a good life? What is ethical living? Is an individual merely the sum total of his/her biological/physical parts or does one have a non-empirical essence some may call soul, spirit or being? To paraphrase one philosophical counselor, when psychotherapists are confronted with such questions they often feel their own inexperience in handling such issues. Generally, in trying to help a person, they reduce such questions to some pathological symptom or consider it as a sign of avoidance in dealing with the more practical affairs of life. Accordingly, they redirect the person from what they believe to be these "depressing" topics. In fact, it was reported by one philosophical counselor that a former president of the American Psychological Association describes philosophical counseling to be harmful. But to date there has been no evidence of its harm. In fact, it raises the question, What is harmful?

For some may think that it is harmful to reduce meaningful life questions to a pathological symptom or have them treated as little more than neural impulses.

However, it is uncertain how this relatively new movement called philosophical counseling will manifest. Will it follow the way of its modern psychotherapy counterparts? For among the many philosophical systems there are those who are the "philosophical fathers" to modern psychotherapies' empirical views of humankind. Some of these schools of philosophy reject the idea that humankind is inherently rational, see it as flawed in some way and thus see reason and rational procedures as ineffective in trying to resolve humankind's problems. On the other hand, will philosophical counseling follow a rational philosophy as found in our third movement?

Our third movement, though not well known, has its beginnings in the early 1950s. Different from philosophical counseling and modern psychotherapies, it follows a rational philosophy whose roots are found in the Platonic tradition.

This movement originated by philosopher and Platonist Pierre Grimes, is called Philosophical Midwifery (PM). It is Pierre Grimes' adaptation of the "Socratic Midwifery" found in Plato's dialogues. Socrates likened his art of dialogue to the art of midwifery, but instead of bringing to birth children, he claimed his art helped bring to birth ideas and beliefs of a person. In like manner, PM helps to bring to birth those false beliefs that one experiences as one pursues one's goals and it does so through reason alone—i.e. through a purely rational approach.

PM claims that humankind is inherently rational in that one's emotional and physical behaviors proceed from premises or beliefs (rather than chemical imbalances or physiological processes), and that they can be seen as understandable. PM further assumes that individuals desire the Good and seek to pursue the good they desire. Accordingly, psychological problems are intelligible because they have a morphology: that is, each problem has a goal, specific steps that repeat in cyclical form with emotional highs and lows, a specific function within the family, and a history with identifiable patterns. Because each problem can be seen to be understandable in terms of the data itself, there is no need to interpret either by way of prescribed behavioral techniques, advice from historical philosophers or any other means.

PM assumes that as one pursues a goal, whether a practical goal or one of a more lofty nature such as the quest to "know thyself," one will inevitably encounter blocks in the form of false beliefs about oneself and reality. These false beliefs are irreconcilable with one's goals, but they demand obedience unless their purpose and function are understood. PM offers a structure to understand the origin, transmission, acceptance, maintenance and dissolution of these false beliefs. It provides the method to uncover and explore what makes the false beliefs believable and why a person would accept something that is false about the self.

Those exploring in this way—that is joining in the exploration of oneself in one's own terms to search for the reasons for accepting false beliefs about oneself—come to realize they sacrificed a rational state for false beliefs about themselves. They realize these false beliefs manifest themselves in behaviors, attitudes and ways of being. Once free of these false beliefs, they can return to a state of being that is both rational and free of conflict.

In the very process of exploring oneself through this purely rational approach, one finds the mind itself to be intelligible and caring and in marked contrast to what appears to be real. Questions naturally arise: Is it possible to make sense even of those thoughts and behaviors we believe to be our most irrational? Is it possible to make sense of those profound moments we have each experienced, those moments of inexplicable beauty and clarity? Such experiences lead us to question: Is there a reality that we all participate in, in different degrees, or do we each have our own reality? What is meant by the Socratic ideal, "to know thyself?" How can one attain it? These kinds of questions bring us to the door of metaphysics.

There are those who find these questions meaningful, and for some such explorations have led them to profound insights into themselves and the nature of reality. They have found in Platonic philosophy a way to make sense of these various experiences, and have consequently returned to study Platonic philosophy not as an academic, logical, scholarly exercise, but as a purely rational spiritual practice that leads to the unfolding of mind that culminates in a vision of the nature of reality. PM functions to help those along this higher path of inquiry by providing the structure to examine the underlying philosophical premises which block one from full realization of mind itself.

It is obvious that those who view humankind from an empirical position would consider such practices impractical and ludicrous and would look upon them with great suspicion—as the medical field looks upon psychologists prescribing medications and as psychologists look upon philosophers getting paid to solve human problems.

For myself, I have found PM most valuable as I explore my most lofty meaningful goals. I also have found it useful in my professional practice. For even in its adapted form as a cognitive/rational psychotherapy, Philosophical Midwifery offers a ray of hope even for those seeking more practical goals, and it brings a new perspective to problems that have baffled and plagued us such as recidivism, serial criminal behavior, addictions, and child abuse, etc.

For further information on Philosophical Midwifery or Grimes Dialectical Rational Psychotherapy use standard search engines.

New Perspectives: Spring 2001, pp. 4, 5, 23

New Positive Psychology: A Science or New Religion?

By Regina L. Uliana, Ph.D.

There are numerous self-help and spiritual books based on anecdotal testimonies, religious dogma, or the laurels of Eastern or Western wisdom traditions. There are also original works, which many of these self-help books reference. Martin Seligman, in his new book, "Authentic Happiness," has introduced what he calls his New Positive Psychology movement to realize your potential for lasting fulfillment. Is this another book claiming the elixir of happiness? Is it a science or religion? And how does Seligman's book compare with others who proclaim similar fulfillments and refer to science? Most notably, the Religious Science movement founded by Ernest Holmes and called Science of Mind.

Reviewing both Holmes' representative work on his movement called "Living the Science of Mind" and Seligman's most recent work "Authentic Happiness," the reader is drawn to ask the most obvious question: What is the relationship of each with science? At first glance, Holmes has proposed what appears to be an oxymoron by referring to a religious science or science of religion. On the other hand, Seligman, a distinguished national and international scientist in the field of psychology, has written on a subject more often associated with religious or spiritual aspirations than with scientific inquiry.

Holmes, in his work "Living the Science of Mind," argues that the science of religions provides a way to affirm a spiritual presence, a consciousness, an organized intelligence that is universal for those who recognize the weakness and unscientific position in religious dogma and superstition and the limitations of an empirical/materialistic world view. He associates with the concept science to make his religion or spiritual path more acceptable to those who may be skeptical of religious dogma. He claims a relationship with science by first calling his movement Science of Mind. And then declares that the Science of Mind studies the natural principles of this spiritual presence, mind or consciousness and assumes that by applying his declared natural principles to the persistent problems of everyday life, an individual can achieve happiness, freedom and a meaningful life.

In essence, he presents his system as a joining of what he means to be science (the "organized knowledge of natural law of mind and its application to life") and religion (any man's belief about his relationship to the invisible universe and his ideas of God, gods or ultimate reality). Holmes's concept of science is used loosely. Because he claims that his principles are natural laws of mind, he assumes he is associating himself with the concept of science. In reviewing his work, it is clear that Holmes proclaims these principles that he believes lead to a revelation of the spiritual presence, rather than discovering these elements through scientific inquiry. Further, it is only through faith of these declared elements that one can attain a realization of mind or consciousness existence, and then one must use this mind or essence of reality in "constructive ways" in everyday living.

Unlike Holmes's faith-based proclamations, Seligman begins his book with provocative research findings on positive emotions to support his New Positive Psychology movement. He then discusses the questions he has had about his own research and with the direction psychology has taken over the past century. He argues that, while psychological research during the 20th century has not been wasted and has brought significant understanding to negative emotions and mental illness and the treatment that provides relief for those suffering from mental illness, the field of psychology is unbalanced if it doesn't inquire about mental health, positive traits and positive emotions.

In addition to the challenge to his psychological colleagues, his second goal is to provide the reader with several findings to support one's use of his New Positive Psychology to realize one's potential for lasting fulfillment. His main concern is to measure the basic elements of happiness—namely positive emotions and what he calls signature strengths—and then tells the reader "what science has discovered" to increase these elements. Of special interest are the several simple, easily scored self-report tests and surveys.

By completing these simple tests, the reader is drawn into the research process and can compare results with findings Seligman presents. The reader can retake the tests if they engage in Seligman's suggested practice to chart changes. Seligman discusses the implication of these findings on the consequences of increasing positive emotions and concludes that, "By activating an expansive, tolerant, and creative mindset, positive feelings maximize the social, intellectual and physical benefits that will accrue."

Seligman argues that, in addition to increasing positive emotions, one must also focus on good character and increasing good character. To discover the elements of good character, he and his colleagues reviewed both psychological literature and writings of the great thinkers and the basic writings from the major philosophical and religious traditions that spanned over 3,000 years and across cultures. They found what they believed were virtues common to almost all the religious and philosophical traditions: wisdom and knowledge, courage, love and humanity, justice, temperance and spirituality, and transcendence. They acknowledged that the meanings of these terms varied among the various traditions. However, rather than reviewing and learning the meanings of the terms and their role within the particular traditions, Seligman and his colleagues decided to redefine them into their own terms.

They believed these virtues and their varied meanings were "unworkably abstract for psychologists who want to … measure these things." To make the virtues applicable to measurement, Seligman interprets what criteria would constitute a behavior or "display" of one of these virtues. He outlines 24 "behaviors," or what he calls signature strengths. He then developed a survey that he says measures the quantity of each of these 24 signature strengths. Readers are provided with this survey to discover their own signature strengths as defined by Seligman's New Positive Psychology. He also suggests that frequent review and practice of these signature strengths increase positive emotions. Parents are provided a bonus which includes a survey to measure what Seligman has interpreted to be children's signature strengths and eight techniques to increase children's positive emotions. Of course, the validity of the surveys can be questioned. For one could question how is humanity or transcendence or the others he mentioned virtues. Further, one could question whether the questions he developed can identify the virtues as described in the traditions referenced.

Holmes also studied many philosophies and religions to find the common elements that he believed were the principles of the nature of what he calls universal spirit or God. However, Holmes relies on the practitioner to believe what he has declared to be the principles and, in believing, must use them to deny ideas contrary to the believed principles. In so doing, he claims the practitioner will realize the presence and perfection of God (page 307). He does not rely on scientific inquiry to verify whether his way has been effective or ineffective. For Holmes, verification is based on the practitioner's personal judgment whether he has realized the spiritual presence.

In contrast, Seligman adds some ways for the reader to measure whether there have been changes if one decides to follow his suggestions. However, this assumes that his redefinitions and these surveys clearly represent the profound fundamental ideas (often referred to as abstract ideas) and thus measure what they claim to measure. In one sense, the reader has to believe that Seligman has represented the virtues in his redefinitions.

Although there are these differences between the two authors, there are also some striking similarities. Seligman does not continue to remain as objective or scientifically neutral as he had in the first part of his work. Instead of providing research findings that show the impact of using his defined signature strengths, something I anticipated, Seligman assumes the value of using these signature strengths and offers suggestions on "how to use these signature strengths in work, love, parenting and having a meaningful life, and then speculates what would happen if they were used in these areas." And like Holmes, who believes in repeating his declared principles, Seligman assumes that through repeated practice of the signature strengths, one has the potential of gaining greater happiness and meaning in one's life.

Seligman's thought is similar to Holmes in yet another way. As we follow Seligman's work to the last chapter, one learns Seligman's religious/ spiritual views. They each now have proposed a religious view to the reader and have associated it in some way to the concept of science or scientific inquiry. But their views are contrary to one another. Holmes assumes the realization of the spiritual presence can be attained here and now, for it is always present to everyone. It is realized by those who have faith in the principles and apply them here and now.

Seligman, however, concludes that authentic happiness and a meaningful life is an ever-evolving process which moves toward omniscience, omnipotence and goodness. Unfortunately, such fulfillment is not possible in one's lifetime due to his assumption that life continually evolves toward greater complexity (page 259). The implication of Seligman's position is that achievement of absolutes, such as authentic happiness, realizing your potential and lasting fulfillment, is not possible. Further, neither developed methodologies or described stages of development in one's pursuit towards greater meaning and happiness. For Holmes, one has a realization or one doesn't, and for Seligman, one can achieve a degree of happiness but not authentic happiness in the sense of an absolute.

Both authors as major spokesmen for their respective fields and movements have attempted to raise the awareness of those who may be skeptical. Seligman has opened the door for inquiry and for his scientific colleagues to address what has been understood in philosophical/spiritual traditions for centuries. He has provided evidence that supports psychological research to redirect investigation towards mental health rather than mental illness. He attempts to broaden the horizons of psychological research, but the methods of investigations may need to change as he has also seen the need for the field of psychology to change its parameters and include the study of mental health. The models for understanding mental health and fundamental ideas are likely to require different assumptions and methods of research beyond the empirical models. But, notwithstanding, Seligman, in recognizing this need to shift, has set a precedent for future research and inquiry. Holmes, in recognizing the limitations of religious dogma, set a precedent for pursuing spiritual quests by associating some kind of scientific inquiry in attempts to verify his ideals and to reduce the force of religious dogma.

In conclusion, the claim of Seligman's New Positive Psychology movement to bring one to realize one's full potential and achieve authentic happiness is not likely. As has been noted, the journey to reach the acme of human potential goes beyond what Seligman has presented, and further, he himself believes it's not possible. Of course it does not mean that such a goal is not possible; we are simply looking at the implications of Seligman's position. There are numerous traditions and systems which express the opposite of Seligman's position.

New Positive Psychology and Plato's Philosophy

Ironically, if either Holmes or Seligman were to have studied the idea of virtue in, say, Plato's dialogues, they would discover that to practice justice is not what is commonly known to be justice, nor are the ideas of temperance, bravery and wisdom. In fact, Seligman's assumption that there are behavioral displays of justice is not how Plato describes the virtue justice in his dialogue the *Republic*. For the virtues of justice, temperance, bravery and wisdom as described in Plato's *Republic* may not be apparent, and the use of these virtues is not for civic or social benefits. Nor is the goal to gain happiness, although the consequences of enlightenment and wisdom are likely to bring great happiness.

In fact, they are used to cultivate states of mind rather than observable behaviors. A careful reading of Plato's *Republic* reveals that these virtues are not to be used ideally for the practical world, but for the spiritual journey of the philosopher king, and that journey is described not for the purpose to rule over a country or state, but to rule and gain a just and wise guardianship of oneself. Further, Seligman would have to learn that wisdom functions not for practical purposes, but defines one who has reached the highest spiritual essence of reality, and that reality is not empirical but can only be gained by reason and contemplation. Similarly, the maxim to "Know Thyself" is not to describe one's autobiography but to discover one's spiritual essences.

To do that as described in Plato's dialogue the *Phaedo*, one must separate one's soul from the body and the senses or empirical world. But Seligman, being an empiricist, would most likely reject the idea of soul and not be familiar with models that understand these fundamental ideas and their impact in their own terms within a tradition. So he has taken profound ideas and made the reader believe that they can be reduced to measurable terms. Further, if Seligman and Holmes were to read some of the spiritual wisdom traditions, the goal to realize one's potential is not gained by increasing one's happiness or through faith but to gain wisdom, to know thyself, to gain enlightenment. The journey is not pleasant and often is described as distressful and conflicted, for one must challenge one's fundamental beliefs, ideas, or assumptions. Both Seligman and Holmes would need to face their fundamental assumptions in themselves and the fundamental assumption of their traditions and their movements and reveal the conflicts in doing so. Also, both have assumed the scientific model is the more ideal model, and neither have challenged whether science is the most ideal model to understand spiritual pursuits.

Further, both of these two positions are contrary to well known wisdom traditions that assume a reality that transcends time and natural laws; that reality is not complex but is ever present, simple, eternal and one; that a complete understanding and enlightenment is possible here and now; and that understanding takes precedence over faith and the sense world. For such a journey, I recommend Plato's *Republic*, Proclus's *Commentary on Plato's Parmenides*, readings from *Essential Plotinus*, Dogen-zenji writings on Being–Time from his work the *Shobogenzo*, The Opening Mind Academy Web site by Pierre Grimes, and Pierre Grimes' and my book, *Philosophical Midwifery: A New Paradigm for Understanding Human Problems With Its Validation*. (See especially Chapters 13 "Comparative Study of the Dialectic" and 14 "The Platonic Tradition and Evolution of Consciousness.")

Regina L. Uliana, Ph.D. is a clinical and research psychologist and a certified philosophical counselor in Huntington Beach, California. Under the guidance of Platonist Pierre Grimes, Ph.D., she sees herself as a serious student of Platonic philosophy and its practice for personal growth, excellence and enlightenment.

New Perspectives: Winter 2004, pp. 8,9, & 31

Roshi Glassman's Zen Approach to Social Justice

Glassman uses his many different roles—teacher, laymen, clown, businessman, and social activist—to express the uses of Zen in all of life. This, at times, can be confusing to those who follow him who expect to see him in a more traditional role.

By Julie Grabel

It's one thing to work and volunteer in the city in which you live, it is quite another to make it a worldwide movement. But that's what is happening with the Zen Peacemakers, the Greyston Mandala and now the Maezumi Institute in Montague, Massachusetts which is about to accept its first participants for a year-long course of study and experience beginning in October 2006. Founded with an organizing principle of dynamic interplay between spirituality and livelihood, it appears that those interested can experience what Bernard Tetsugen Glassman Roshi calls "the realization and actualization of the interconnectedness of life," and he's not simply clowning around.

Roshi Glassman is fulfilling a promise he made to his teacher. He is dedicating the Maezumi Institute to Hakuyu Taizan Maezumi in gratitude. Here's most of what Bernie had to say in our recent telephone interview:

JG: What track, which includes Zen, Social Enterprise, Peacemaking, Multi-faith and Arts, of the school do you think Maezumi Roshi would have the most difficulty with? And why? Is that a fair question for you?

BG: Sure. But I don't think he would have difficulty with any of the tracks.

JG: Alright. I'm wondering, I guess it's the Arts track…

BG: His mother is an artist; his uncle was an opera singer. He has a brother who taught sculpture at a university in Tokyo. He himself was a calligrapher. He did Japanese archery. His family is very much involved in the arts.

JG.: All right. So you see that as an integral part of life—if all five of these tracks are followed…

BG: It's interesting that you would think that would be an issue because in Japan, Zen was so integrated into Japanese art. In this country we're integrating. There is some of that, and when we think of Japanese Zen, it involves poetry and calligraphy; it involves the arts because its core period was so integrated. Now, I am trying to bring integration of Zen into social action in the business world. *That* wasn't so much done in Japan.

JG: OK. So the social action aspect then—do you see yourself as being at the forefront of something we could call a social justice movement?

BG: I am not sure if I am at the forefront, but I am one of the pioneers in that work, I would say. I think that's certainly fair to say.

JG: Do you think you are in any system at this point, yourself?

BG: Well, I'm a clown. And one of the things a clown might do is juggle. I don't see myself as being in one place or another but in many places at the same time, and I have emphasized this, but an emphasis at different phases of my life on different things and people have noticed that emphasis. But the one thing that I think is constant is that I love creativity and change, so I am always looking to push my own boundaries, but the sphere I like to work in is pretty broad. I made a vow back in 1976 that I would work in all aspects of life.

JG: I am struggling to understand the relationship between what you do and Buddhism—where the Buddhism is. I guess where it stops or if it stops. Do you see it throughout everything you do?

BG: Yes. Maezumi Roshi always emphasized that Zen is life, and I always emphasize that. It's life. It's all of life. There is nothing in life that is not part of the practice. Now what is the essence of the practice? For me the essence is the realization and actualization of the wonders of life, of the interconnectedness of all things. So, if you accept that as my definition of Zen, or of Buddhism, which I mean, I take from Shakyamuni Buddha, it's not a new definition. But I emphasize that. So, if that's your definition, what aspect of life is outside of that?

JG: Right!

BG: So, what you bring to the work that you do is whatever aspect of society you're working in—you try to bring the realization and actualization of the interconnectedness of life. And that can affect how you do your corporate work, how you do your social action work, how you do your religious work. It affects how you do your art, it affects everything.

JG: So, the people that you expect or hope to come to the Maezumi Institute—are you hoping that these people will take what they learn and go back to their communities and do large things?

BG: Large or small—my hope is that their life moves towards the interconnectedness of life. I want people to go back to their various activities and bring the dharma into that, and by dharma what I mean is the interconnectedness of life. Not the particular form that arose to teach that; I mean the essence itself.

JG: Can you talk about loving action and healing and how those are related in your work? I see they are related, aren't they? I see that sometimes it's referred to as loving action and other times I think you are talking about healing.

BG: Yeah. Well, when you say Loving Action, you are referring to our third tenet. So, I say that the actions that arise out of nonduality…now, it's a technical term, so I use the State of Not Knowing and Bearing Witness to be representing this nonduality. For me, if you can come to a situation with a state of not knowing, then deep listening and deep openness, and no attachment to a fixed idea. If you can come that way and then bear witness to the situation, that is, eliminate the gap, the subject-object gap between you and the situation, if you can do that, then what naturally arises is loving action. You don't bring ideas of yourself to the picture, in general, you're just doing things. And so that means you've really entered the place of deep listening to yourself because that's what you are—and you're bearing witness because that's what you are. You're not saying, now I move my hand to here. It's a very nondual situation. If you get hungry, if hunger arises, you reach for the food, if that's the loving action, it arises naturally. If an itch occurs, you scratch it. It's not a process of rationalization or debate of the thing. It's the spontaneous reaction. If you're sweating you might fan yourself. Those are all immediate loving actions. So, if you take that to the whole world, it is the same thing. If you could come from that place of complete openness and go into a state of bearing witness of becoming the situation, loving actions will arise naturally.

JG: And, of course, that would be a very healing thing for our planet.

BG: Yes.

JG: I see how those are related.

BG: Yes, what is the probability that if you're hungry, you're not going to get yourself food, or if you're tired, you won't rest? Those things can occur if we have a sickness, but if we're healthy, they won't occur. It is the same with the planet. If we're healthy, we'll take care of things with loving actions. And, vice versa, when we're not, there is something unhealthy going on, and one of the biggest illnesses is with the ego, or the separation between self and other.

JG: What does a person do who wants to be a Zen Peacemaker, who is attempting to be this integrated person and runs into difficulties or blocks? I can hear Maezumi Roshi screaming, "Go sit!" But what do you do?

BG: I am starting a year long training program in exactly that. It's called The Zen Peacemaker Training Program in which we are teaching a lot of tools—lots of tools that we have found over the years to be helpful both to the individual, to working groups and in society. That's part of our Peacemaker Track. But it's the gist. We're starting a yearlong certificate program in that. It's starting in October now. We're going to be actually bringing people from Japan next March, but we're going to start for Westerners in October.

JG: I see that you are traveling all over the world. I would expect that you would meet people that would hopefully come to your institute. Is that part of your goal to find these Peacemakers around the world?

BG: I have been working for a long time around the world. There will be people coming here. You know, to come from Europe to where we are is cheaper than to come from California!

JG: When you took off the robes to go and *bear witness* to homelessness, I'm assuming you reconciled your Zen principles and I know we have talked about that a little already. I know you didn't leave your Zen principles behind, but it seems like you would have had to do some changing ...

BG: I took off the robes for two major reasons. The most important is that I wanted to put more emphasis, or help legitimize the role of the lay person to Zen person to Zen practice. The Zen practice that I inherited, or I was a part of, is the Soto sect. In the Japanese Soto sect, the only legitimate Zen practitioner is a priest. And that's not true for many other Zen groups, or religious groups. And it's certainly not part of the teaching of Shakyamuni Buddha or of Mahayana Buddhism in particular, so I wanted to be a role model as a lay person.

JG: Oh! Thank you.

BG: And I wanted to come into the questions you're raising ... You're implying that when I stepped down I lose something as a Zen person, as a priest, and I wanted to show that as a lay person I am as bona fide as any priest in knowledge and practice of Zen.

JG: So, you're actually gaining by…

BG: I think I did. So part of it is that I was trying to bring that message to this country, that a lay person is not second class to a priest.

JG: I appreciate that. What is your second reason?

BG: I had pretty much handed over all of the Zen center temples that I was in charge of. I had handed those over to other people. So I wasn't functioning as a priest. I was functioning as a Zen teacher, and as a roshi. I was still teaching Zen and I was using my Zen to bring it to social action arenas and business worlds and various other worlds, but I wasn't functioning as a priest officiating at services and doing those kinds of things. So, no need to wear the robes. I still had a temple and wanted to be in charge of that temple. I am not talking about a zendo, a Zen center, but more a temple. A temple needs a priest, but a Zen center doesn't. I'm using the word temple to mean the place where you have human spiritual work done and the meditation hall where you have your Zen training.

JG: I don't have any more formal questions for you at this time. Do you have anything that you would like to say to New Perspectives readers that I haven't touched on, or that I have left out?

BG: No. It feels good.

JG: You have good energy. You are certainly presenting a way for people to help society and with it, a structure from which people can move out of and into their communities.

BG: Great. Thank you.

JG: Thank you.

Julie Grabel was manager of the Open Mind Academy in Costa Mesa, California from 1999 to 2004, and manages the openingmind.com Web Site.

New Perspectives: Summer 2006, pp. 20, 21 & 27

Section Two: COLUMNIST–PHILOSOPHER

The Noetic Study

Whatever occupies your mind, you become.

By Pierre Grimes

Before any beginning there was and always will be Mind. Whatever is and whatever becomes is simply because Mind ceaselessly unfolds its richness before itself. It is only those who have turned their minds away from an interest in other things who are able to know the Mind. The matter is, after all, simple: "Whatever occupies your mind, you become." The images and thoughts we experience weave together an image of the self which we then act out. The difference between becoming this or that and knowing the nature of the Mind is a quantum jump. Those who can be said to truly live are those who are nourished by the Mind, since it is by participating in Mind that one begets Mind and Truth.

The existence of Mind is called real Being. It is through the intellect that we recognize the power of Mind and its wondrous scope. So too, it is the activity of Mind as Intellect that brings us to that startling experience of being bathed in the splendor of Beauty, and so discovering that this is the source of our existence we acknowledge that this is what discloses that life is worth the living. Entering into and mingling with true Being we gain an access to what we knew we always were. Yet we are astonished by its brilliance and by the realization that we are that very reality.

Those who can chart that kind of a journey are the true navigators of the soul for they can guide the soul to its destination. Once we desire to become true lovers of that kind of knowledge, we move away from the base opinions of the many, and we strive to chart our way through the difficulties of self-defeating beliefs that deny our heritage. Cultivating a real understanding that turns us about and prepares us for visionary knowledge, we enter into that life of true philosophy that culminates in opening the mind to its own reality. The source of all divinity is Mind and it is the object of all strivings. Yet there is more to this than praising the Intellect's seeing because, within the richness of this experience, it is possible to make distinctions which have become the basis for those hierarchical principles of metaphysics so dear to the Neo-Platonists and that have been personified as gods by the Platonists.

Knowing is transformative, and since the noetic is seeing with and through the mind, it is the noblest art. It is the Platonic Art that can offer us an opportunity to emerge out of Plato's Cave into the upper world. It is a journey that forces us to confront those beliefs that have made us loyal to the images reflected as shadows on the wall of the cave. It is no easy task since it means we must train the mind to pass to the full vision of the upper world by seeing the necessity to move out of belief, and from understanding to pure knowing. We are never alone on such a quest because once we start along this journey we are open to influences that help us along the way. However, in another way we are never alone because we are *not* that thing that stands alone, but what embraces the cosmos.

New Perspectives: Spring 2003, p.17

The "Why" Question

All we need is a few "ifs" and ... unfold a greater mystery.

By Pierre Grimes

We enter into a strange and forbidden arena when we ask, "Why do we have the problems we have?" For that question raises another question that is as strange as it is necessary: "Could it be that this existence of ours is designed for us to face our problems?"

Surely it is a difficult question to answer properly. But, while we ought to know when an answer answers a question, it is not at all clear that questions like these can be answered. It may even raise a doubt about our ability to answer such questions. This doubt may mask a taboo, a taboo against exploring such questions.

However, if we know everything else about our existence but have failed not only to appreciate the depth of these two questions but also to answer them to our satisfaction, then everything we know is shallow and without much meaning. Still, that means there are answers to those questions. How important might these answers be? Well, what if that failure to answer these questions means we have lost our connection with the nature of Reality?

Now, if we can find some way to connect our questions with the theoretical sciences, then we might avoid the need to speculate; however, we know that is not likely. So, there appears to be no alternative other than to enter the realm of speculation, even though we will only be left with probable arguments. Yet they may lead us to a few arguments that just might offer us a possible explanation to this mystery. All we need is a few "ifs," and with them we might discover and unfold a greater mystery.

Thus, we must be bold enough to say that if it is necessary that we have the problems we have and they necessarily bring us to states of suffering and anguish then there is no justification for them if they are not solvable. If this is so then we occupy an unjust universe, a universe whose very fabric is flawed. To be pained and suffer unjustly can only be attributed to an unjust cause since we know of no crime that we have committed yet we suffer needlessly. If our reasoning is sound how can we avoid the terrible conclusion that if there is a God we must wonder if that God is unjust or indifferent to our suffering?

To go further in our speculations we need to pick up another "if," since we have seen where the last one goes. What if there was a way to solve our problems and suppose that with such solutions we can gain an understanding of how we came to have our problems in the first place?

Well, if this is possible then we can say something different about our universe. For if we can no longer liken it to a torture chamber or jail, then we will need a kind of learning about oneself to solve the problems we have—perhaps, a school of some sort. Still, that leads us, inevitably, to another why question. "Why was this universe of ours designed for learning if we are only here once?" Well, let us assume that justice requires sufficient reincarnations until one learns to rid oneself of all our problems and once free of them to come to a realization of the nature of the self. Why? Because if this is a just universe then knowing the self will give us an insight into the nature of our reality as being just and good, and that surely takes more time than one has in one lifetime.

Well, this leads us to conclude that it would only be just if in knowing oneself that we discover our own nature is divine and that our existence here is the school for our souls to enter the divine. But what is the way to know thyself? It has been said that philosophy is the love of wisdom, a wisdom divine that is no stranger to knowing the self. But could the cleansing of false belief be wisdom or is it the preparation for wisdom?

New Perspectives: Winter 2004, p. 11

Should Platonism Replace Modernism?

By Pierre Grimes

Moderns are those who announce with an air of certainty that it is only what can be clutched in one's hands and seen with one's eyes that is real. They try to persuade us that only those ideas that have their source in common everyday experience are meaningful. They want us to distrust any reflection that goes beyond the narrow bounds of sense experience.

The moderns feel that reason and understanding are too weak to sustain any lofty flight of the mind. They heap abuse upon Platonists who say ideas and mind truly exist. Only feelings, they claim, can be trusted, so ignore reason. Since feelings are so immediate and vivid, they ask, "Who can deny what is experienced so intensely?" So they love and struggle oblivious to the need to understand their life. They nod in agreement when they hear "There is no better view, only different viewpoints." These moderns are convinced that even their own theory is nothing more than words that summarize their experience. It is as if their theory is merely a kind of peg board to hang facts upon. However, since they believe their theory leaves nothing worthwhile out, they feel confident that what they say is complete and logically sound. They have no need for any ethics and strive only for absolute power like Dick Cheney and Karl Rove in politics. They violate the sovereignty of nations as they fight wars for profit and suppress the truth behind a screen of lies, as the Downing Street memos exposed the lies Bush told the American public to justify a war over oil. Moderns boast that all one needs to follow is the rule of the jungle; for only the fittest should survive. As for science, they only tolerate it just so long as it provides them with a technology to dominate others, and for products that bring them profit—all the while ignoring the pollution that follows in their wake, like Bush's trade policies. The modern then easily includes materialists, empiricists, relativists, pragmatists, logical positivists, and even the post-moderns. These post-moderns are still moderns since they see the limitations of modernism, yet sink further into it by becoming absurd in their denying what little reason there is in the moderns. The post-modern stuff can be easily composed using an essay generator which "spits out paper with ease" that have the appearance of post modern essays: *www.wikipedia.org/wiki/Postmodernism.*

Now, all this frames an indifferent attitude towards others, since as a modern they regard as primitive any culture or age that does not contribute anything significant to their own needs. They believe this present age is the summit, the fulfillment of history, and so rooted in common sense that any change could only be a fall and bring about a dark age. They study the past to show its weakness, to glorify their present. They use history as a source for literature, and in entertainment they are like Disney productions that live only for the moment's pleasure and is then forgotten. Narrow and bleak is their vision and it is, of course, spiritually hollow and empty.

But what if Homer's "Iliad," a 2800 year old work of the ancient Greeks, contains a more superior vision of man than anything in modern psychology? For recent philosophical studies have shown that Homer's "Iliad" not only took on the question we all ask—"Can the worst among us ever learn to be a noble being with integrity?"—but he also answered it. Homer chose Achilles because he was the worst among the Greeks, and he became the ideal for an age. Achilles' ruinous wrath swept him along a path of folly that brought death and needless suffering to many. We learn that he had to purge himself of all his false beliefs, he had to challenge and reject his own culture's values and most importantly the traditional teachings of his clan before he could truly live the ideal. We learn from these studies that Homer presented Achilles' life with such profound excellence that it includes scenes rivaling the transfiguration scenes of Jesus, and surpasses those of the Bhagavad Gita's Arjuna.

Our belief in modernism has blocked us from seeing that the essential nature of man is one, and that our destiny can only be accomplished when we become fully human ourselves and give up our treasured false beliefs.

However, it might be asked if the weakness of modernism can also be shown in mathematics and logic. George Cantor demonstrated that ideas, like infinity, truly exist and are not mere conventions, and that the idea of God is a necessary idea in the study of transfinite numbers. Kurt Godel put a stake into the heart of modernism when he showed, contrary to their hopes, that modernism can never become complete because there will always be truths that can never be included in their theory. Thus, the loud boasting of modernism is empty of meaning; and while they may still exert an influence on culture, they know they have lost their credibility before the more rational among us. The moderns have so thoroughly dominated our culture and our institutions of learning that those who have learned to appreciate the profound nature of Platonic thought had to reclaim a lost heritage, and these have become part of a new and genuine Renaissance that is taking place around us.

New Perspectives: Fall 2005, p. 27

Is a God a God or is a God a Theos?

One sacrifices the innocent; the other sacrifices what one needs to get rid of and keeps what is needed for one's growth.

By Pierre Grimes, Ph.D.

There are two different ideas about the nature of God. One is shared by the Zoroastrian, Islamic, Christian, and Judaic religions. These are called the Armageddon religions by philosophers since each believes that we are in the midst of a terrible cosmic war between Good and Evil that is right now reaching its final cataclysmic stage.

The war has been going on since the very dawn of time. It is an unconditional war for the total domination of the other. In the end of this fierce struggle all life will perish and the entire cosmos will be consumed in flames, leaving behind nothing but charred remains scattered about in a dead cosmos. Satan is said to direct the forces of Evil, as God is said to be sovereign and leading the forces of good. If God wins he will banish into an eternal Hell all those who opposed him, as well as those innocent nonbelievers who had not taken sides in the struggle.

These irreconcilable forces also struggle within the soul of each of the believers. The struggle is between good and evil, over doubt and disbelief, and over desires and pleasures. The struggle in the soul is a reflection of this war in the heavens between God and Satan. The Earth is believed to be the battlefield because here it is said that creation began and where the first humans, Adam and Eve, have been exiled.

Indeed, the test of the faith of these Armageddon religious believers is that they knowingly must sacrifice life for their God. The model for this sacrifice lies at the foundation of their religion and it is called Abraham's test of faith.

Belief is a curious thing. There is no particular sensation or feeling that accompanies accepting a belief as true. Nor is there any particular experience a believer can point to, to confirm that what they believe is actually believed by them. The content of the belief must be taken literally, no need to search for its meaning. Hence, they need a test of their faith, or of their belief; otherwise they do not know if they truly believe their belief. Their God does not know either or he would not have required a test. Consider Abraham's grief over his willingness to sacrifice his son which gave his God the evidence that Abraham believed, which in turn gave Abraham assurance he believed because the grief he felt is painful and that gives a sense of vividness to what otherwise would be nothing.

The willingness to plunge the world into a total war, to sacrifice innocents, is the price the believer is willing to pay for the test of his belief. To accept and be responsible for the death of innocents makes one an accomplice to murder—be it a man or a God or Satan. Each requires the support of believers and is dependent upon them for their victory. Again, each lacks the skill and wisdom of the perfect general since neither has been able to end the conflict or bring about peace. Thus, since both God and Satan are intent upon destroying all life in their total war, there is no difference in the way that either functions so we can ask: Which is good and which is evil? The root of the word *God* is sacrifice.

The other idea of God is ancient Greek and it is called a *theos*. By way of contrast the Greek God, *theos*, is said to be Good, and the good are said not to be the cause of evil but rather of only good. Evil is in the human realm not the divine and it occurs when there is a conflict and misunderstanding of what is good and beneficial.

The Theos lacks nothing if totally good and thus can not be dependent or lack anything including wisdom. Their model for sacrifice has its origin in the myth of Prometheus, and like all Greek myths it is necessary to grasp the meaning behind the tale. In the myth, Prometheus taught Man to sacrifice by preparing two offerings to Zeus: one, fine cuts of meat disguised as inedible and the other, the inedible, disguised as fine cuts of meat. The inedible was cast into the sacred fire and the other to enjoy as a festival. The meaning is that we must sacrifice what we want to get rid of, sacrifice what we hate doing, and keep what is for our own nourishment and growth. This kind of belief needs no reassurance, no sacrifice of innocents, no religious war to test whether or not one believes or not, because it is rational to assume a God as Theos is Good and has no share in evil. The root meaning of Theos is said to be derived from the idea of running or movement, as the heavenly planets move in their orbits. Which then shall we believe, a God or a Theos?

New Perspectives: Summer 2006, p. 25

Is a Just State Possible?

Or would we first have to become just ourselves before we sought to impose some arbitrary standard on others?

By Pierre Grimes, Ph. D.

Let us assume for the moment that it is possible to construct, if only in theory, a just political state. Further, if we add to it and make this idea of a just state as ideal as we can make it.

Consider that even if it is not possible to bring it into existence it might still be worth the while to visualize what a just state might be like. But what if it were possible to bring this idea of a just state into existence? Well, if it were possible then we could go on and ask, "Are people ready to pay the price for a just society?" Now that raises a curious issue because it might even require us to play some active role in its realization, might it not? So how much would we be willing to add of our own work and sweat to make our society ideal?

In some societies we might have to be careful about even talking about this ideal. We know that to try to bring it into existence in some states would be dangerous, wouldn't it? Perhaps, before going too far in our search for answers it might be important to ask, "What are the forces that would oppose such a just state?" Now that is another curious issue because it might require us to be willing to oppose these forces. They would most likely crush any effort to construct a just state if they thought it would deprive them of their fortunes and power.

In our society it might be that most people might just laugh and ridicule even the idea of discussing this issue because many of them might have been convinced that it is futile to even raise such issues. They would likely sneer at us for not knowing that since there can be no agreement among mankind about what is justice and injustice, any effort to pursue this issue is the height of foolishness. Yet it is not obvious that it is foolish because we all can point to examples of injustice. Surely, if we were to line up the examples of injustice before us we could find some common theme that underlies these terrible acts and use that commonness as a standard for injustice. We could do the same for acts of justice, couldn't we?

Rather than debate the issue let us invite those who would like to join us to create standards for a just society to come together to discuss it. We could do it over the web. After we formulate a standard, we could use it and then we could measure all political systems and determine the degree to which they are just. We could give them grades, a kind of report card. We could even review the programs and plans that each government has for the realization of justice in their own countries and grade the plans once we saw the human cost to implement those plans. Naturally, we could also give poor grades for any act of injustice the government sponsored or committed.

With such a study we might be able to map out the forces that oppose justice and show how they have benefited by acts of injustice. We could draw up an accounting of the deeds of the unjust so that all could see how much they have gained from their unjust deeds. It would be a strange bookkeeping, for it would show the suffering others must pay for the fortunes of the unjust.

There are several things we might do after forming such a list. We might have an interest in visiting those just countries and avoid the unjust ones. Public action might naturally arise from the publication of our study. Wouldn't it be interesting if people withdraw all support from those who transgress the standards of justice? A kind of general strike could be called to withdraw all support to those who oppose justice. If such were the case it would have to be done justly, wouldn't it? Then if we found countries that commit crimes against humanity they could be brought before an international tribunal and forced to face condemnation for their acts.

Care to join in this effort to design and bring about a just society? Or would we first have to become just ourselves before we sought to impose some arbitrary standard on others? Would we first have to decide if being just is really good, or should we trust that being just is good? Now suppose we first have to see the connection between being just and the good before we can be sure that being just is good?

New Perspectives: Summer 2007, p. 25

Regarding a Rational and Just Society

Can we help design a rational and just society?

By Pierre Grimes, Ph. D.

We are like men on a raft who have no idea of the need for navigation charts or like witch doctors who have no idea of the causes of health and disease; and because of that, we have no confidence in our ability to make things right. We know injustices occur all around us; and while we believe some are justified and some not, we have no clear idea of the causes of justice and injustice. Our tyrannical VP Cheney and King George justify war with cooked intelligence; they stock the justice department with right wing Armageddon Christian lawyers, and the corruption is so dense it is difficult to pick on which one to expose. We feel powerless to oppose the insanity of the super rich stacking up more riches as they outsource everything, robbing the treasury and calling it tax cuts, looting the social institutions and intelligence agencies and calling it privatizing, creating think tanks to design strategies to fool us, and manipulate voting machines to steal our elections out from under us. They create terror among us and call others terrorists. We as a people according to the most recent polls want to impeach them both. But where is the ground swell of public opinion that shouts in the streets against their absurdities?

As a people we are silent and frustrated because we lack the will to fight for what is right and don't believe there is a way out. Our schools avoid controversy and are afraid of the wrath of the churches if they openly explore controversial ideas. We have been taught to fear philosophy so we cast it aside like ignorant mariners who can see no value in navigational charts. We are taught that each person has their own unique and personal view of what justice and injustice is, but are not told that this is sophistry from an ancient Greek, Protagoras. So by this shallow and foolish line of thinking we are brought to conclude that no one has the right to say what is just and unjust without imposing their own personal view on the world. For when it is asked, "Who is to say what is right or wrong?" the answer, like in any field, be it sports, music, or anything else, is that only the person who knows the difference between the right way and the wrong way to do anything is the judge and no one else. When they taunt you and say, "What seems true to anyone is true to him to whom it seems so, so it is all relative to the observer," you can say, "sure that is true for things one observes because each person does view things from their own viewpoint, but we are not asking about *seems* so but what *is* so."

Our teachers are taught this nonsense in our universities as a way of ending students' voicing their opinions in classes, since teachers are instructed to avoid controversy. Our educational system was guided by the doctrine of the separation of church and state, so churches keep out of politics and the schools won't challenge their teachings. It is a surrender of the opportunity to bring students into the use of the mind. Now, however, it is all over since the churches have declared a war against secularism and have taken control of our present corrupt government and stuffed school boards with true believers. So the deal of separation of church and state is dead in the water. Schools can now advance a rational approach to the teaching and advance critical thinking, and that is the very thing that believers can't stand. What will happen now that the Bible can be part of the school curriculum? One thing is certain and that is if it is taught like any other subject it will be seen for what it is because without the Bible thumping believers scaring people with visions of hell it will be just like another dull subject taught by an indifferent teacher to restless pupils. The teachers who approach Bible study with well accepted historical criticism will leave the students laughing in the aisles. They will chuckle at the foolishness of that old Protagoras doctrine, and spend their time on preparing to enter the most serious questions of our age: Can we help design a rational and just society? Can we map out the forces that have always opposed justice, equality, and fraternity among all of mankind? What would we gain by living in a just and rational society?

New Perspectives: Winter 2008, p. 23

Justice and Reason in Our Leaders

Leaders who ignore the need for justice in the State realize that liberty and reason are their worst enemies.

Pierre Grimes, Ph.D.

Throughout the ages mankind has had a dream that one-day Man will assert himself in the spirit of freedom and come together to craft and bring into existence a just society. It is no easy task because while it requires focusing on how to remedy the inequalities and injustices it also means we have to give up tolerating injustice within ourselves, our families, and our communities.

However, we know well in advance that those we accept as leaders will always urge us to forego our dreams to realize justice because, as they argue, we face some far more serious, pressing and immanent dangers. If we persist in holding to the priority of our dreams we know our leaders will scream aloud that there is a necessity to sacrifice those dreams and with it our freedom for the good of the whole. Leaders who ignore the need for justice in the State realize that liberty and reason are their worst enemies. It is not in politics alone that we see this hideous force unleashed upon our whole society. We are taught to ignore the destructive policies that create and exploit injustices in government, business, education, and the military. The drive to exploit and control the earth's resources brings with it terrible injustices. The theft of societies' resources and its institutions is covered by the name "privatize," and that high sounding name covers the violence done to one's fellow man, to nations, and to the Earth. Privatizing is theft for personal gain, and it can only be achieved by silencing the opposition to this high crime. The many have suffered as the few have gained vast wealth and power, but these few are like mindless bloated corpses floating down the river of time. Those who acquiesce to this absurdity have lost the chance to stand against the irrational. In opposing the injustices we affirm our own rationality, and in joining with others we can express a collective will against injustice. Whatever is thought to be above the law is itself lawless. Any law that protects injustices has no binding power over rational beings nor does it have authority to overrule reason since law should reflect reason, as reason is the source of law.

When the demands of reason protect society from injustices they are called laws, and as laws they enshrine mankind's right to protect oneself and society from injustices, so they stand as a bastion in defense of freedom and in opposition to injustice. The government that invades another and tries by their acts of violence to steal another's resources, be it oil, or slaves, functions as a hideous criminal enterprise and should be brought before the courts of international justice to be tried and condemned for their acts. The laws of reason are simple enough and express themselves simply: no profit should be made from war, and those who do so shall forfeit any gain. This is no different from laws that state that it is right to confiscate money and materials gained by those caught dealing illegal drugs.

Governments that block from the media news critical of their doings and provide tax breaks for their friends and the most wealthy should lose their right to govern. Equally the corporations that subvert the political process by buying off politicians through campaign contributions, gifts, and by establishing themselves as tax shelters must lose their legal right to be a corporation. International financial groups that subvert the national sovereignty of nations and undermine economies of states must be brought before the courts of reason to defend their pernicious betrayal of reason. Banks that "money launder" illicit money are part of the same group of thieves and should be treated accordingly.

There is nothing new here, it reflects the principle that is enshrined in the Ancient Hellenic vision of reason and law. Whenever historical circumstances permitted these ideals of reason and law to flower it brought about society's reawakening, a Renaissance. There have been several renaissances; each had its day and each was brutally destroyed by those who fear the free expression of the life of the mind. It is by returning to our ancient heritage of freedom, reason, and law that we will shall once again see a return to the mind's flowering.

New Perspectives: Fall 2008, p. 23

Section Three: NEWS STORIES

International Community Gets a New Perspective on Consciousness: Philosophical Midwifery in Russia

By Julie Grabel, C.C.
Administrator at Academy for Philosophical Midwifery

While the world's athletes competed in the Olympics in Australia, I attended what might be considered an Olympics of the mind at the Eighth International Symposium on Philosophy and the Theory of Culture in St. Petersburg, Russia. The topic this year: Intellect, Imagination, and Intuition: Reflections on the Horizons of Consciousness. The title of the symposium evoked images for me of the world's experts on consciousness being able to demonstrate the highest states of mind as they shared their vision. As Administrator of the Academy, I wanted to see first hand how a group of international philosophers interested in consciousness would respond to Pierre Grimes' presentation on Philosophical Midwifery (PM), since the practice of PM brings us to reflect on our highest personally significant goals and how to achieve them with excellence which necessarily cultivates higher states of mind. As the Russian people move into capitalism and open their doors to outside influences, consciousness becomes a particularly appropriate topic of discussion among international philosophers in this place of extremes. Freedom from false beliefs may provide the conditions for meaningful activity to emerge from the pregnant silence, and it is exciting to be a part of the birthing process.

Philosophical Midwifery has been introduced to the international community at other conferences and many people have been attracted to its beauty. This time scholars and students from around the world, including the Chair of the symposium, Liubava Moreva, Director of the St. Petersburg Branch of the Russian Institute for Cultural Research, and Dr. Massimiliano Lattanzi of UNESCO's Division of Philosophy and Ethics, gathered to share views of consciousness. Following Pierre Grimes' discussion on the transmission of the pathologos, a sick belief which becomes the driving force behind our view of the world and ourselves, there was a very spirited dialogue which will be worth reading in the Proceedings. Many of the participants understood the role of analogy in Pierre's work and asked meaningful questions about social pathologos and how to remove it. Understanding is the key to its removal, but the image of removal makes me think of an exorcism while, in fact, the dissipation of the block is accompanied by a release of energy and the attainment of excellence, the effects of this type of seeing. Several presenters at the conference emphasized suffering and horror from which people emerge into freedom and creativity. Perhaps those who are familiar with struggle may not be blocked from the effort it takes to understand ourselves and can sustain the level of puzzlement and struggle required to understand the pathologos, but as Pierre said at the conference, "Let popular culture recognize that what they really fear is opening up to a higher reality, an *ontos*, Being."

Through my discussions with some of the participants at the conference I could see that they tended to think in terms of collective consciousness and group goals and that to think about personally significant goals was new and intriguing to them. One of the interesting challenges for the Russian language is in discussing ideas such as The one or The Good since Russian does not have a definite or indefinite article. They can make these distinctions by talking about good in itself or beauty in itself but it isn't clear that they see such a thing as beauty in itself since their idea of beauty is defined by the consensus opinion, the collective view. One woman who teaches philosophy in Russia was moved by the prospect of pursuing something personally meaningful as she talked about herself and her own goals as well as those of society as a whole. She was among a group of people interested in a demonstration from Pierre, and so he took seven people through a PM exploration at the same time, using his usual set of questions. Each of us wrote our answers out privately and participated at whatever level we could engage in at the time. PM guides us to see that when we are blocked, we experience a particular state of mind which can be traced into our personal history. One of the participants shared the impact it had on him to discover that he had been in a particular state of mind during his presentation and that he recognized it as a problem and that he remembered the same state appearing in other analogous situations in his life, and it was in reflecting on his own experience with PM that he could understand part of what Pierre was talking about.

My interest in what we humans are doing here and how to do it with excellence continues to challenge me in my work at the Academy, and I look forward to continuing an international dialogue.

New Perspectives: Spring 2001, pp. 46 & 47

Milestones and Remembrances

Birthday

Pierre Grimes celebrated his 80th birthday on November 19, 2004 at the Women's Club in Huntington Beach, California with members of his Noetic Society and others. He was born on November 16, 1924. He has taught philosophy at Golden West College in Huntington Beach for 38 years.

From his first article in the Yale Journal QJAS (Quarterly Journal on Alcohol Studies) in 1961, where he outlined a philosophical dialectical approach to the study of alcoholism to his book in 1998, "Philosophical Midwifery: A New Paradigm for Understanding Human Problems," he founded and has remained in the forefront of the philosophical practice movement. This movement has taken various forms in many parts of the world, and many Europeans see Gerd Achenbach as founding the movement in 1981, but it first emerged in Southern California when Pierre formed the Noetic Society, Inc. in 1978 and directed its Philosophical Midwifery program. Pierre Grimes' work challenges the fundamental structure of contemporary thought and culture and presents us with a new paradigm.

For the Zen master, Alan Watts, he was a Jnana Yogi, "that is to say, one who comes to an authentic realization, or *satori*, by an intellectual rather than an emotional or physical discipline."

At 79, he traveled to Europe twice. He gave his paper, "Homer and the Struggle for Excellence," at the first World Olympic Congress of Philosophy, held during June 27 to July 4, 2004. In November of 2004 he was at the University of Liverpool, England for a conference called "Philosophy as a Way of Life." His paper was "Philosophical Midwifery: The Rational Structure of Pathologos Problems, Dreams, Fantasies, and Meditation."

New Perspectives: Winter 2005, pp. 37, 42

PROMETHEUS TRUST NAMES NEW NORTH AMERICAN DISTRIBUTOR

By Julie Postel

Thomas Taylor is without a doubt the most prolific translator of Platonic works to ever benefit mankind! His years of translating in the 19th century yielded enough material to fill 33 volumes. Those of us fortunate enough to be studying Platonic Philosophy with his translations sing his praises and toast his generosity and insights into Platonic thought, for it is not often that we find any other translators who demonstrate an understanding of not only the Greek language, but also the Hellenic spirit. His consistency in translating the highest metaphysical language in a way which brings us to the most profound understanding is not only useful to us, but also beneficial to reaching the highest states of mind open to man. Now all of Thomas Taylor's works are available in the USA through Opening Mind Associates, the new North American distributor for Prometheus Trust.

When I began my studies with Pierre Grimes in the late 80s, Thomas Taylor's translations of Plato's dialogues were not available in any form other than a bound set put together by Garland Publishing in 1984. One of Pierre's students, Rod Wallbank along with his wife, Sarah, had been making these and other texts of Plato's works available by searching the used book stores of the west—sometimes traveling great distances to see a text that they heard might be available. They shared any extras with fellow students by hosting holiday parties where they would pass on what they had gathered throughout the year—sometimes I walked out with 20 books. After several years, many of the Noetic Society, Inc. members ended up with good libraries for studying Platonic philosophy. But in order to read Plato as translated by Thomas Taylor, we had to read the Garland set and every s was typed as an f—a feature that we quite quickly and surprisingly adapted to reading correctly. But when Rod discovered a group of Platonic philosophers in England who were beginning the project of publishing all of Thomas Taylor's works, he began a decade-long relationship with Prometheus Trust. Rod would gather the money from interested Noetic Society members and would arrange to get us all the first volumes of their Series. The money from those sales made it possible for Prometheus Trust to print the next volumes. The cycle of printing, selling and printing more volumes continued until all 33 volumes were made available to the public including translations of the complete works of Aristotle as well as works from many other philosophers such as Iamblichus and Porphyry.

When the Series was about two-thirds complete, Prometheus Trust found a distributor in the USA, Robert Clark's Minerva Press, and the availability of these wonderfully hardbound purple books was expanded to others. In the transatlantic dialogues, Rod Wallbank discovered that his copy of Taylor's translation of Pausanias' Guide to Greece was not even in the hands of the Prometheus Trust Group until he offered it to them for publication and this material became Volumes 31 and 32 of the Series. When the Internet began making all of these relationships electronic, Prometheus Trust expanded its range of influence. And when the owner of Minerva Press decided to retire, it was natural to pass the torch of distributorship to someone in the Noetic Society, Inc. Opening Mind Academy, Minerva Press, and Prometheus Trust. Since this author had been working with Minerva Press, it was my pleasure to import the books directly from Prometheus Trust, and the Web site http://www.openingmind.net is now providing access to their entire catalogue. There is more information on the Thomas Taylor Series on the Web site http://www.prometheustrust.co.uk and the reader can also find out more about those studying these works by visiting http://www.noeticsociety.org.

Opening Mind Associates exists to promote the work of Pierre Grimes, the Director of the Noetic Society, Inc. Pierre has been our guide in understanding Platonic thought and his love for Proclus brought us into contact with Thomas Taylor's translations of some of Proclus' commentaries (also available in the Thomas Taylor Series by Prometheus Trust). Therefore, the new OMA also offers all of Pierre Grimes' works, a short work by Robert Clark and also the rest of the Prometheus Trust catalogue which includes works by Tim Addey, among others. It is with great pleasure that OMA also offers Pierre Grimes' DVD catalogue of 115 lectures and demonstrations, making it more certain that future philosophers will have access to these valuable study guides.

New Perspectives: Winter 2008, pp. 44-45

Section Four: FILM and DVD REVIEWS

The Bleep Movie

Reviewed by Pierre Grimes, Ph.D.

A recent film asks "What the bleep do we know?" However, before answering the question a few things should be said about the film. First, the film won the Platinum Houston World Fest Film Festival award; it received the Audience Choice Award for "Most Thought Provoking Film" at the Sedona International Film Festival; and it gained distinction for being the Audience Award Winner for Best Hybrid Documentary at the Maui Film Festival. As a result it has sparked an interest in the Ramtha School on Enlightenment because it is said that this school was the philosophical and spiritual source behind the film. Surely, a lot of people acclaim it.

Secondly, the film itself includes a mix of 14 authorities from quantum physics, religion, and metaphysics. On the spiritual side the film presents itself as a vehicle for the great 35,000 year old mystical sage Ramtha, who speaks through J.Z. Knight, his channel. He is reported to have been channeled saying, "Welcome to the kingdom of heaven without judgment, without hate, without testing, without anything." The science side is shared with Alan Wolf, Amit Goswami, and Masaru Emoto, and others, but the interesting quantum view they present is that reality is alive, fluid, and with unlimited pure potential. Surely, a lot of authorities support it.

What shall we say to such an assemblage of witnesses to the truth they proclaim? There is no point in questioning their credentials or the data they have presented in the film. We should only keep our eye on the message of the film and reflect on the assumptions that guide the making of the film. So then let us assume that what they say is true and wonder why it has received the positive response.

Surely, the voice of these physicists reporting the subatomic view of reality indicates a reality of vast unlimited possibilities while the spiritual side of the film offers what is thought to complement that view with the Ramtha revelation that there is no need for judgment or for testing. Combining the idea of infinite possibilities with no need for judgment nor testing we now have the usual New Age mantra that everyone can have their own private truth with no worry about testing or understanding since judgment has been abolished.

What do we have here but aphorisms of the old Greek Philosopher, Protagoras, "what seems true for anyone is true to him to whom it seems so" and "who is to say who is right or wrong since everyone has a right to their own view." These aphorisms are always rejected as foolish whenever some tragedy or crisis occurs; because it is then that we wake up from this foolishness and seek those who know. Otherwise we might never get out of our troubles. At these times, who listens to those who say and believe and that there are no better views and that everything is relative to the observer? Thus, it is that you can always get people to applaud and give honors to what they already believe if you dress up an old belief with fancy embroidered robes. By the way, the film does have a creative animation sequence in it that you might enjoy, and there are parts that are thought provoking even if they are doubtful.

New Perspectives: Winter 2005, p. 30

Big Mind/Big Heart Revealed

The Big Mind Program

By Diane Hamilton

Reviewed by Julie Grabel

In this DVD the Director of The Big Mind Program, Diane Hamilton, introduces us to Zen Master Genpo Merzel Roshi who has been wanting to share Big Mind with others since 1971. When he became interested in the Voice Dialogue approach in psychology which was developed by Hal and Sidra Stone, Genpo Roshi integrated what he learned there into his process called Big Mind. In the DVD, he leads a group through the stages of a process which shows us how to see the self as one with everything, but also to appreciate its apparent parts which are not separate.

One of the participants from the DVD set "Big Mind/Big Heart Revealed," said that some people find introspection scary and "it helps to have a guided tour." But it was clear to this viewer that most of the participants in this session led by Genpo Roshi had previous experience with Buddhist meditation and were familiar with the terms for each part of the Self which gets "called up" in order to gain more clarity of their function. By separating out what has been determined to be a finite set of qualities of the Self, each person gets a clearer view of the parts, and then when instructed to experience higher states of mind, the individuals see their unity and to the viewer watching, in some cases a transformation is witnessed. But there is little sense of discovery on the part of the individuals until the more advanced states of mind are discussed. Even though the participants appeared to be sincere, it seemed to be more of a re-enactment until one participant shared her struggles with maintaining Big Mind as a state of mind and Genpo Roshi worked with her to bring her to a deeper realization. It is interesting to me that all of these people are sharing their experiences out loud on tape, a very unconventional thing for Buddhists since most of this type of dialogue with a Roshi would normally take place in the privacy of the one-on-one interview or dokusan. It is unusual for the higher states of mind to be shared with those who may not have had these experiences before—it has always seemed to me to be more of a "club" for the serious Zen student. The descriptions in this process match the literature, but also appear sincere in the moment, especially as they reach the higher states of mind. One of the most profound states is called Dropped Off Body and Mind and when Genpo asks his students what it was like to experience it; no one should have said a thing!

When he calls for the Integrated Fully Functioning Human Being, we can see that the participants are in a relaxed and yet energized state of mind and one of the participants describes it as the "ability to access whatever is needed" and the freedom and effortlessness are contagious. There is nothing wrong with the Self, it simply confuses itself! Ken Wilbur says this process allows one to "glimpse the awakened mind." Since our society is not accustomed to watching one another be introspective and put words on our experiences, it is charting new territory to prepare this DVD.

The Lenz Foundation made it possible for this DVD to be produced, but the relationship appears to end there. Gratitude is expressed for the resources which make such good work possible.

New Perspectives: Summer 2007, p. 11

A Documentary on How We Were Led Into the War with Iraq

No End in Sight

Review and commentary by Pierre Grimes, Ph.D.

Here is a "must see" film by Charles Ferguson. The title says it all, "No End in Sight." It puts our problem right in our face. It is a vivid presentation of the most hideous example of man's stupidity and arrogance ever recorded. It lays open what amounts to criminal negligence. The war machine rolls on crushing one state after another, next it is Iran if it is not stopped. Ferguson's documentary lays it all bare. The picture he puts together of Iraq and Afghanistan is a lucid and devastating, uncompromising picture of Bush's war, but as a documentary it is a failure. First let me set it straight by saying that Ferguson did a masterful job by stringing together what desperately needs to be seen, but many authorities before have cited what he presents in the film. You can check it out in a whole list of insider books at your local bookstore and web based news, such as *www.truthout.org*.

The shock of the film is that what few have known was going on is now laid bare for all to see. So, what is new? Well, (We now have people coming forward who were in the chain of command willing to tell the truth,) such as former Deputy Secretary of State Richard Armitage, Ambassador Barbara Bodine (in charge of Baghdad during the Spring of 2003), Colonel Lawrence Wilkerson, former Chief of Staff to Colin Powell, and Iraq civilians. But, what does this mean? It means that while they were on their jobs they did nothing to call the Bush story lies, and now they tell the truth. Sad isn't it that they didn't have the courage to say it out loud to us all when they were in positions of power. Sure thing, it is Bush's war, sold to us as our right to get revenge against the terrorists for the terrible destruction of the twin towers of 9/11.

Why call the film a failure? Maybe it is and maybe not. Is a documentary a failure if it doesn't disclose the truth? Should a documentary leave the larger questions not even asked? The film raises questions in the mind of the viewer, but doesn't ask them. What the film does is great and for what is left unexplored or stated suffers a failure.

Let us ask a few of these questions and raise a few issues. Let us ask these: Is this Bush's war? Were Weapons of Mass Destruction found? Was Saddam Hussein supporting the terrorists? The answer to them is, No. Some might say that the "terrorists struck us, we didn't strike them." So, we went to war against the terrorists and took the war to Afghanistan, right? No, you are wrong. Why: Well, if some criminals terrorize their victims, does that make them terrorists? Those who struck down the Twin Towers are not just criminals, but international criminals, since 17 of the 18 on those planes were citizens of Saudi Arabia. No one would accept the idea of going to war against criminals. Wars are fought against nations, armies have to win wars and occupy the vanquished people. Had Bush told Americans that the UN must form an international police force to hunt down these international criminals then the world would celebrate his vision. We would join those who marched in support of us all over the world, including 100,000 who took to the streets in Iran's capital, Tehran. It would have saved hundreds of thousands of lives from a terrible unnecessary war.

Where would funds come from to support a war against truth? At least one source is clear: according to a new Government Accountability Office report, the Bush administration in just two years, 2003-2005, spent $1.6 billion of our tax dollars for these experts—the PR firms, think tanks, media consultants—to "spin," to disguise simple truths and make believable the lies and distortions of his administration. Christopher Lee wrote the story in the Washington Post.

As the film sets out for all to see, the plan to invade Iraq was plotted well before 9/11. The issue is not whether or not we should have avoided all the costly mistakes of the Iraq war, but whether we should have been there at all. The point is that there was a program of massive deceit to spin it so Americans would believe it was just to invade Iraq. The fraud is well documented in Ambassador Wilson and Representative Conyers' work, *George W. Bush Versus the U. S. Constitution*, as they lay out the infamous Downing Street Memo that uncovers the deception, manipulation, and cover-ups of this war and Bush's illegal domestic spying program.

The Bush gang's philosophy is clear to a small group, and you can check the web to see it for yourself. Google the *New American Century*, stare at their dream of conquest, and for a shock notice all those who signed that declaration. They want us to become the new Rome, the new Empire. Nice isn't it since they never asked if we want our young men and women to be dying for the glory of the military industrial complex, which President Eisenhower warned us was the real threat to our democracy. Militarism in every country, if left unchecked as it is in this country, brings a halt to freedom and makes of us the target, the "blowback"; see Chalmers Johnson's *The Sorrows of Empire*. The war machine of Bush's White House was woven out of the oil lobby, gun lobby, the Christian conservatives, the Dominionists, inspired by those seeking the rapture with the Armageddon. These Christian Dominionists thought they could force the hand of God by inflaming the Middle East in War and that would bring about the end of all life on this planet. These Dominionists plot and act towards making the U.S.A. a mere device to further their dream for another Crusade against the infidels. See Michael Weinstein's truly shocking expose of this nightmare at www.militaryreligiousfreedom.org. They have an authoritative political model that is narrow in its vision and destructive to most Americans' ideals. See John Dean's "Conservatives Without Conscience." The multinational corporations create a wave of hostility against our true Democratic image since they steal natural resources from nations by fraudulent lending. See John Perkins' "Confessions of an Economic Hit Man." There may be no end in sight if we check on Scott Ritter's "Target Iran." The evidence is mounting that Iran will be hit next because the evidence is there that our three carrier groups are now threatening Iran.

We need to determine if there is evidence to bring all these people to stand up and defend themselves, we need to view all the evidence, and we can only do this if we take the responsibility and act. Each of us should do what we know we should do. Should we ignore the radical fundamentalist church's role? Do they need saving? Should you make sure your vote counts? We jail our kids for smoking pot but are we afraid of sending the polluters, the war criminals, and the profiteers to jail?

New Perspectives: Winter 2008, pp. 35 & 51

Section Five: BOOK REVIEWS

Reality: A Matter of Just Seeing

How the World Can Be the Way It Is: An Inquiry for the New Millennium into Science, Philosophy, and Perception

By Steven Hagen

(Quest Books; 343 pp.)

Reviewed by Julie Hoigaard, Ph.D.

Steve Hagen's *How the World Can Be the Way It Is* is fun reading for anyone with a little familiarity with Buddhist teachings and quantum theory, for (by numerous examples) Hagen shows how much of the *dharma* of Buddhism is in accord with quantum theory and perception. Several major thinkers in consciousness, Buddhism, and quantum theory are cited over the course of the book including Zeno, Nagarjuna, Aristotle, Shakespeare, Gödel, Polanyi, Gleick, Penrose, and more. Each of the 10 chapters begins with a quote about Reality from Buddhism, literature, or philosophy which is then substantiated within the chapter by a quantum theory. The examples are clear and concise. Hagen's purpose through it all is to make a case against "belief" and "conception" and a case for "perception"— pure and simple.

Throughout the book Hagen cites many instances of the *conception* of Reality, running headlong into the *perception* of it in order to show how the two are incompatible and necessarily paradoxical. Filtering our perceptions of the world through our conceptions of the world necessarily entails paradox. We make a fundamental mistake when at the instant after "just seeing" we tell ourselves what *we believe* we're seeing and then perceive Reality through that conceptual filter. If we could "just see" Reality, says Hagen, without first interpreting it through our system of beliefs, we would be most rational and at the "end of life's sorrows."

Because of unsettling paradox, we hold on to *common sense*, a thinly disguised version of a world otherwise abounding with paradox. "Common sense is no more than our habit of artificially packaging Reality so that we might keep contradictory premises from ever sharing the same territory." Yet, when common sense conceptualizations encounter Reality, familiar contradictions abound. So why not dump quantum theory? Hagen asks. Because, he points out, quantum theory is the most successful theory in science and accepting it forces us to embrace ontologies which our common sense finds absurd.

With each chapter the reader encounters a popular commonsensical position ("belief habit") as well as a relevant quantum theorist/quantum discovery. The common assumption of *past and future* is readily challenged to the point of impossibility as Hagen draws forth Bell's Quantum Theorem of Interconnectedness. With this, the reader sees clearly that only Here and Now is the Reality. Hagen brings in the theories of Einstein to make the point that Reality is not concept, and not paradox or confusion. As Einstein discovered that time and space are relative to the position of the observer (Relativity Theory), so too when we can learn to see Reality as a "thorough going relationship by dynamic relativity" and not as static, unchanging objects, then paradoxes no longer occur at all.

"So what should we do?" Just See and act accordingly. We're reminded of Bohm's statement of the universe being an "... unbroken, wholeness of flowing motion ... [where] observer and observed are not distinct ... " Hagen concludes by telling us that once you just see (without reliance on belief or intent) you'll be liberated and most rational as will be the world.

New Perspectives: August/September 1996, p. 53

A Model for Exploring Personal Questions

Philosophical Midwifery: A New Paradigm for Understanding Human Problems with Its Validation

By Pierre Grimes, Ph.D. and Regina Uliana, Ph.D.

(Hyparxis Press; 309 pp.)

Reviewed by Robert Apatow, Ph.D.

Paradigm shifts occur in a discipline when a new theory is presented that answers questions previous theories were unable to solve. In doing so, the new theory transforms the entire discipline, recasting what is accepted as the legitimate research methods, educational models, questions and answers in that discipline. The two most famous paradigm shifts were the shift from the geocentric universe to the sun-centered universe, known as the Copernican revolution, and in this century, the shift from the Newtonian to the Einsteinian paradigm in physics, sometimes called the quantum revolution.

In "Philosophical Midwifery" Dr. Pierre Grimes and Dr. Regina Uliana present a new paradigm for human understanding. However, they are not seeking to solve scientific questions, they are offering a model for exploring human questions, the personal ones each of us possess about our particular life. Their remarkable claim is that the problems each one of us face not only can be solved, but that they can be understood. In other words, they are claiming that karma is rational.

The central thesis of the work is the following:

> "It is entirely possible to verify for oneself that we are part of a caring and intelligible universe. The verification is a kind of proof since it is a way of understanding that is based upon a realization that our mind constantly communicates with us and for our benefit. The communications from the mind are as profound as they are utterly appropriate to our circumstances; for while the scope of the mind is pervasive, its precision is always directed to what is personally significant. We will demonstrate that our choice of goals, the problems we face, the daydreams or fantasies we have, and the dreams that visit us in our sleep each and every one of them are like doorways into the richest source of insights into our life. What we discover through these insights is that the mind itself provides ample evidence of its own goodness and intelligibility." (page 18)

Grimes has proceeded on a long intellectual and spiritual journey to reach this vision of man and the universe. In his first chapter, "The Way it All Began," Grimes describes how experiences as a soldier in World War II led him to reflect on the reasons for decisions on the battlefield that cost his friends' lives. His journeys led him into relationships with some of the leading thinkers of the twentieth century: Alan Watts, Joseph Campbell, and Albert Ellis. Grimes also studied with many leading Zen teachers and became the dharma successor of Korean Zen master, Myo-Bong. However, it was Grimes's experience as a psychologist in a Salvation Army center where he discovered that a Socratic approach to therapy—called Philosophical Midwifery—was the key to unlocking the root cause of personal problems.

According to Grimes, at the core of human problems is what he terms the pathologos, which means "sick belief." The pathologos is a negative belief that is passed down through the family and functions in our lives as a "psychic parasite." Perhaps the most challenging aspect of Grimes's view is his claim that all families possess sick beliefs. The pathologos "is the cause of much of the chaos experienced in our life" and manifests itself most clearly when an individual strives towards his or her highest and most personally meaningful goals. Therefore, human beings as individuals and as a race must free themselves from these "sick beliefs" in order to achieve excellence.

According to Grimes, this is the fundamental goal of human life. Although this particular work will give the reader much to reflect on, it is not a "self-help" book. (Grimes has a computer program called "To Artemis" and an unpublished workbook that serve this function.) "Philosophical Midwifery" is the culmination Grimes's lifetime of research into the nature of human problems. The work presents a thorough account of the nature and structure of the transmission and function of the pathologos in human beings, a scientific study to validate his claims, and a comparative study of Grimes's approach with other cognitive systems (these psychological studies are the main focus of Grimes's coauthor, psychologist Dr. Uliana). As well, Grimes devotes chapters to the discussion of chaos and field theory in contemporary science which he sees as offering accurate models to describe the functioning of the human psyche in the grip of a pathologos.

New Perspectives: Winter 1998-99, p. 24

Looking for Truth Instead of Right or Wrong

The Spiritual Art of Dialogue: Mastering Communication for Personal Growth, Relationships and the Workplace

By Robert Apatow, Ph.D.

(Inner Traditions; 195 pp.)

Reviewed by Barry Goldberg

There are a lot of self-help books out on the market, but few approach the challenges of life in such a way as to connect with the depths of ancient wisdom. What is remarkable about "The Spiritual Art of Dialogue" is that it does just this in a manner that is both accessible and appropriate to the real needs of modern life.

The primary aim of the book is to introduce a framework for communication that avoids the pitfalls of argumentation that we all know too well. Dr. Apatow uses his focus on dialogue to delve into every aspect of personal and spiritual growth. The basics of the approach that Apatow presents come from Socrates, the philosopher of ancient Greece, and are expressed with a simplicity and obviousness that are the hallmarks of real truth. In dialogue, says Apatow, we need to focus on a question, seek the truth, work together as friends, and follow the *logos*, the Greek way of really listening. The Socratic approach to dialogue works very differently from ordinary arguing or debating; Apatow explains it is like a game in which two people take on the role of questioner and answerer. This is the key to avoiding the war of words. Each person takes his or her turn presenting a position while the other person takes on the role of a Socrates and seeks to evaluate the position through questioning. The beauty of this approach is that it gives people a way to work together during discussions instead of working against one another. According to Socrates "we enter into dialogue not to win but to seek the truth." When we are at one with the truth we gain genuine self-fulfillment.

I can share with you from personal experience that this approach is very powerful and effective. It helps us get to the core issues and roots of disagreement. I have been in business meetings in which all hell was about to break loose, and by following the simple principles of dialogue presented in this book I have been able to maintain clarity and objectivity to allow a resolution to emerge naturally from a challenging discussion. This is what is so beautiful about dialogue. It is not an artificial process. It is a natural path to let truth come forth not as the possession of one party or the other but as the consequence of the process itself, and for the benefit of both parties.

Apatow devotes a large part of the book to explaining the nature of the human drama that often makes communication so challenging, especially in the area of romantic relationships. In these challenges, Apatow sees the greatest opportunity for growth and intimacy. I have often known that true communication demands the courage to break out of roles and to see through the way we sometimes project on one another. In my own life this has been a challenge that has brought the greatest rewards, because to me a deep and intimate dialogue with someone I love has the power on the intellectual level that can sometimes be as profound as intimate, physical union. Apatow has put into words an ideal of communicating and relating to one another that can bring us to the self-fulfillment we all long to achieve.

Barry Goldberg is the president of Imajika Health Products, Inc.

New Perspectives: Autumn 1999, p. 36

Tolstoy's Search for Meaning in the Major Religions

The Wisdom of Humankind

Translated, Condensed and Introduced
By Guy de Mallac
(CoNexus Press; 224 pp.)

Reviewed by Robert Apatow, Ph.D.

What is true religion? According to Leo Tolstoy, "True religion is based on our love for God, and it focuses on how we should act—treat others as you would have them treat you. Follow the simple truth of love and refuse to follow all that is false. We become happy only when we serve others and not our own selves. True religion is based on the constant striving to achieve this level of love…"

The search for meaning and the truth of religion are an important part of Tolstoy's great works, *War and Peace*, *Anna Karenina*, and *The Death of Ivan Illyich.* The last seven years of the great novelist's life were dedicated to a work of nonfiction; a book entitled *The Wisdom of Humankind.* In this work, Tolstoy presents his understanding and personal expression of the essence of the world's philosophical and religious traditions.

Each of the thirty-one chapters begins with a succinct statement of a universal theme such as "Faith," "The Spirit Within," "God," "Love," etc., and then continues in a short chapter that discusses important aspects of the key theme. The final chapter, for example, is titled, "Life is a Blessing," and begins:

> Our life and its blessedness (happiness) consist in closer union of our spirit with God and others from whom it has been separated through the body. The union is reached by the spirit as it reveals itself through love, and frees itself more and more from the body. As we realize this, life then becomes constant blessedness in spite of all misfortunes, sufferings, and ailments.

Tolstoy's religious quest began in his own Russian Orthodox tradition, which he later found limiting. This experience led him into a brief period of agnosticism, but his faith was eventually renewed in part by his appreciation of the authenticity and sincerity of the faith he witnessed in the peasants of his time. Throughout his life Tolstoy studied all the world's major religions,

Christianity, Islam, Buddhism, Taoism, Confucianism, and Judaism, often in the original languages.

This edition of "The Wisdom of Humankind" by Guy de Mallac is the first new translation of the work since 1911. For readers today it will help to make more widely known why, as one scholar notes, "... Tolstoy was at one time regarded as the conscience of humanity, the greatest single moral force in the world during the last years of the nineteenth century." Indeed, Gandhi considered him as his own mentor and guide in the path of nonviolence.

Guy de Mallac taught a course on nonviolence within the Peace Studies Program at the University of California at Irvine from 1970 through 1994. He became Professor Emeritus in 1995.

Robert Apatow is a philosopher, counselor, and the author of "The Spiritual Art of Dialogue: Mastering Communication for Personal Growth, Relationships, and the Workplace."

New Perspectives: Autumn 1999, p. 37

Maezumi Roshi's Influence Continues

Appreciate Your Life: The Essence of Zen Practice

By Taizan Maezumi Roshi
Foreword by Bernie Glassman
Edited by Wendy Egyoku Nakao
and Eve Myonen Marko
(Shambhala Publishing; 144 pp.)

Reviewed by Julie Grabel

"Even though you are in the midst of the awakened life, you do not realize it."

Maezumi Roshi did. And he spent much of his time encouraging others to transcend duality. Bernie Glassman, the first dharma successor to Maezumi Roshi says in the forward to this exceptional book that Maezumi Roshi's goal was to bring the dharma to the west and that he "received authorization to teach from three different teachers in three different Zen lineages..." The richness of Maezumi Roshi's teaching, therefore, reveals that the vastness and depth of his intimacy with the literature from which he draws the examples he uses in his formal talks is as unsurpassable as the Buddha way.

As Wendy Egyoku Nakao says in her preface, "These teisho are not ordinary lectures, but are intimate communications from master to student." She says, "The way to read this book is to eat it one bite at a time." Whether you read it all at once or one teisho at a time, this book can be read at any point in one's practice. The reader will be able to identify with Maezumi Roshi's talks and each time they are read, we see less of ourselves as we think we are and more of what really is. The way the material is organized in this book is brilliant, showing a beautiful progression of ideas and it is particularly helpful to see quotes from one teisho explained and understood in another. As an example, the editors have selected talks where Maezumi Roshi repeats well-known Dogen stories in different teaching contexts and at times uses his own translations of Dogen's work.

After reading this work, Pierre Grimes, one of the first Americans to sit with Maezumi Roshi, had this to say:

> "Death is a curious thing because it is expected that one's presence ends with one's death. For whatever truth there is in that, I must add that for some people this is not true. Maezumi Roshi was one of those men whose presence even now does not seem to me to have died. Perhaps, all I am saying is that my own sense of Maezumi Roshi has not died because I learned that the way he was able to smile at our folly and what seemed so important to several of us lingers on in a strange timeless fashion.
>
> "Some years ago there was a discussion going around about the difference between spiritual experiences and LSD experiences. As I recall, these discussions never solved the issue. Talks went one way and the other much like the slight wind tossing the leaves around in the fall. Why sit if you can drop acid? Why not compare them and see which gets you not only higher but just what are the upper reaches of LSD?
>
> "So the talk went and sometimes it turned on the question of the user because it was asked if we could find the ideal subject, the one most receptive to the acid, what would their trip be like? Could it be compared with some enlightenment experiences? What were the most profound trips from one of these six-to-eight hour trips? Was the highest acid trip a mere makyo, or illusion, or mere nothing?

"Now, we all knew the ox-herding pictures that describe and depict eight stages of enlightenment and the questions arose again and again, "Where would the highest acid trip be ranked among these enlightenment experiences? Who might be the best subject to test it? And, so the discussion went on.

"Well, a group of us from the Huntington Beach area used to drive up to the L.A. Zen Center to do the sesshins and during one of them a couple of the young women with us hit upon an interesting idea. Since they were often asked to serve the Roshi his tea during his formal lectures, the teisho, at these sessions, wouldn't it be interesting to drop in the tea pot a cube of LSD. They did it.

"We all sat diligently and so, too, did the Roshi. We sat and he sat. He sat exactly as he always did. He quit exactly at the right time, walked around like the rest of us, returned to sit again just like the rest of us. We wondered if he just might get upset after learning he was on a trip. The worries increased, the time went on.

"The evening sitting session was over, the winter breeze was coming through the zendo and when the bell announcing the end of the sitting rang, the roshi got up from his cushion and looked my way and said in a quiet voice, "most beautiful makyo ..." and he went his usual way with that smile which we all knew meant that there was more to Zen than dropping acid and maybe not even as good as watching the falling leaves."

New Perspectives: Spring 2003, pp. 50-51

On Zen Practice: Body, Breath, and Mind

Editors: Taizan Maezumi and Bernard Glassman
(Wisdom Publications; 208 pp.)
Reviewed by Julie Grabel

What is old, is new again. Originally published as the very first publication by the Zen Center of Los Angeles (ZCLA) in 1976, this reissued edition stands as a compact collection of dharma talks and commentaries by many of the greatest teachers of Zen. It functions as an all-in-one sampler, an excellent companion for the serious Zen student, new or old.

The new preface by Wendy Egyoku Nakao, the present Abbot and head teacher at ZCLA, and John Daishin Buksbazen, assistant teacher at ZCLA, prepares the reader for the simplicity and clarity of the teachings which might have been difficult to grasp in their original oral form. As stated in the original foreword by Robert Aitken: "... multiple themes, even disparate views, form the tapestry of correct Zen teaching."

If you could only have one book with you from which to build a Zen practice, this one could do it for you. Whether you are honoring your teachers by reading their talks or learning how to bow and why, you won't be disappointed. Taizan Maezumi's talks are the most numerous in this collection and his commentary on Dogen Zenji's "The Way of Everyday Life" is especially inspiring and clarifying. This book contains a nice glossary and a listing of "Zen teachers who have received Dharma transmission in the lineage of Roshi Taizan Maezumi," as well as other helpful appendices.

Pierre Grimes was among the first Americans to sit with Maezumi Roshi. When asked about those early days, Pierre said:

> "One unusual foggy day some years ago I recall Maezumi Roshi discussing with a small number of us that he did not think Americans would respond favorably to the idea of a sesshin. The idea of sitting for many days on a cushion accepting Zen discipline was something he wondered if Americans would take seriously enough to try. One of our group said, "Just try it and you'll see.' In those days Maezumi Roshi had three monks who served him and took care of the single house on Normandie in L.A. and they too accepted the challenge. Armed with Kapleau's "Three Pillars of Zen" and the Roshi's talks, we sat and learned that it is in the everyday way of being that the divine manifests itself while being just what it is. What was started

in those days in doubt has become the mark of Maezumi Roshi's legacy and is witness of the enduring good he started and that others have continued. It was a good day that day."

New Perspectives: Spring 2003, p. 51

Lopez's Story of Buddhist Practice

The Story of Buddhism: A Concise Guide to Its History and Teachings

By Donald Lopez

(Harper Publishing; 275 pp.)

Reviewed by Michael Cox

Donald Lopez has built a career on borrowing the postmodern spirit to reframe the Western representation of Buddhism. So it is of interest when he takes off his critic's hat and attempts to give us his vision of Buddhism, as he does in his new book, *The Story of Buddhism.* As the title suggests, the spirit of his prior works infuses this one: Lopez is careful to point out that this is "his story" of Buddhism and as such is going to be different from other approaches, such as an economic or anthropological perspective. In his view, there is no one universal Buddhism but a collection of communities that have existed in various times and places who have identified themselves as Buddhists.

However, Lopez is willing to say that a general picture of Buddhism can be constructed from these various Buddhisms. To do this, he focuses on those aspects which he says are common to all forms of Buddhism—a cosmology, the Three Jewels, monasticism, the laity, and enlightenment. Through these aspects, he weaves a skillfully articulated history of Buddhism that is informed by recent scholarship—such as the reexamination of the relationship between Theravada and Mahayana—and draws on examples from the stories and practices found in India, Thailand, Tibet, China, Japan, Sri Lanka and others to animate his picture. In this picture, Buddhism is not primarily about philosophy or doctrine, but about "practice." This includes various types of meditation, but also death rituals, pilgrimage and the relationship of the sangha and the state. In many ways, *The Story of Buddhism* can be understood as an extended introduction to Lopez's *Buddhism in Practice*, which also attempted to shift the focus away from the philosophical orientation of many Western introductions to Buddhism towards an emphasis on its everyday lived traditions.

In this sense, *The Story of Buddhism* is not simply the "outsider's" version of Buddhism, as opposed to the "insider's" version that one finds in the writings of Robert Thurman with whom Lopez is often contrasted. It might be better understood as a history of Buddhism from "on the ground," one that attempts to present the many different ways in which Buddhism has been practiced and utilized as opposed to a presentation which represents Buddhism from the perspective of only its elite practitioners, such as Nagarjuna or Tsong Khapa

New Perspectives: Spring 2003, p. 52

How to Raise an Ox: Zen Practice as Taught in Master Dogen's Shobogenzo

By Francis Dojun Cook
Foreword by Taizan Maezumi Roshi
(Wisdom Publications; 177pp.)
Reviewed by Julie Grabel

Zen Master Dogen's writings are fundamental for the Zen student, especially those of the Soto form which Dogen established. Dogen's work has been translated from Chinese to Japanese and then into English and many have written about their understanding of his greatest work, *The Shobogenzo*, but according to Maezumi Roshi, Dr. Cook's translations and interpretations can be solidly relied upon by both scholar and practitioner.

Dr. Cook's goal is to make Dogen's teaching accessible to those of us in the West and to make it possible for us to understand "what it means to practice Zen." This reviewer believes he has succeeded in illuminating Dogen's work for East and West. His style is simple, straightforward and elegant, mirroring the principles of the practice he clarifies for us. No wonder that the original 1978 publication by the Zen Center of Los Angeles has been reissued for us now since there is a growing interest in meditation.

What is the relationship between mediation and wisdom? What is Samadhi and does it come to us in our everyday mind? What is "The Way" and what does Dogen tell us about our practice? These and many other questions can be pondered through this work. Dr. Cook has provided several essays of his own on the Zen of Dogen, and translations of many of Dogen's talks. There is also an added bonus of genealogy charts of Chinese Zen Masters so that the reader can get historical reference points for the various people that Dogen references.

This work can assist you in deepening your understanding of Zen practice and is an excellent tool for the serious student of the Soto form.

New Perspectives: Spring 2003, p. 51

DAMIANI WRITES: "...THE SENSIBLE UNIVERSE IS THE PRIMORDIAL SCRIPTURE."

Astronoesis: Philosophy's Empirical Context • Astrology's Transcendental Ground

By Anthony Damiani

(Larson Publishing; 393 pp.)

Reviewed by Cary Costner

Astronoesis is a brilliant re-extension of ancient but perennial Neoplatonic thought into the field of astrology. It's the sort of book of wisdom that a real Harry Potter would be given by a real wizard, but it's not likely to be a best seller. Only some souls yet "affine" with the reborn "wisdom school" and the intellectual rigor of its sacred mysticism and magic. (Here's a clue: it blows your mind while nurturing it.) It requires sober study. It also helps if you innately thrill to the idea that the entire sensory universe is all offspring of the contemplative exuberance of Divine Mind. It also requires knowledge of astrological symbolism.

Damiani proposes to show that the metaphysical terms of Plotinus (the great 3rd Century Neoplatonic sage) are expressed in the symbolism of astrology and therefore our cosmos and our lives. Damiani writes that he will show that the sensible universe *"is the primordial scripture ... it embodies the wisdom of the primal principles which are beyond it."* Surprisingly, for those who are already convinced of the reality of astrology and of Plotinus' metaphysics, *Astronoesis* accomplishes this. Damiani does show that the astrological symbols express the metaphysics. At the very least, this approach to astrological symbolism provides a visible model for the content of Plotinus.

Personally, Plotinus has always amazed and inspired me. However, I'm not yet convinced of astrology's claim that the position of the stars and the planets, per se, really tell us about ourselves. When the chart works, I currently believe that it is because of nonlinear dynamics or synchronicity, not unlike the *I Ching* or *Tarot*. I am convinced that there is some way that the universe delivers meaningful things at the very moment we need them. I'm just not sure that it hinges on the location of the planets.

Frankly, I think synchronicity conjoined me with this book. I got this sudden impulse to drop in on an old philosophical friend whom I hadn't seen in ages; unlikely, given her schedule, she happened to be at home. A day later, she was unexpectedly contacted by the editor of this magazine who needed someone to write a review of this unusual work about Plotinus and astrology. So I came home to find this strange request on my answering machine. Now, it had been several years since I had any appetite for metaphysics, but only recently I had started to feel a new sense of the sacred in the ordinary life. So I agreed to take a look, and the book was mailed to me.

In a very timely manner, synchronicity had provided me with a fine vehicle (Astronoesis) and a productive context (writing a review) for a possible rapprochement with metaphysics and astrology. After wrestling with some unanticipated philosophical biases, I finally got into Astronoesis. It's a fine work and very highly praised. The Dalai Lama described Damiani as "*a truly great man ... one of my closest spiritual brothers.*" Paul Brunton, Damiani's teacher, described him as "*a philosophic genius ... a fully qualified philosophic teacher.*" Robert Hand, whom I know to be one of the most respected thinkers in astrology, wrote that *Astronoesis* is "*possibly the most important book on Philosophy and Astrology and the Metaphysics of Astrology in the last 1500 years.*"

Brilliantly conceived, the structure and method of Astronoesis follow the fourfold structure of Plotinus' metaphysics. The sections are structured around the four terms in Plotinus: the One, Being/Intelligence, Soul and the World. The method has the following four stages: 1, each of the four sections is studied for its essential idea (One); 2, each section is viewed in terms of its parts (Intelligence); 3, the first two steps are then extended into the terms of astrology (Soul) ; and 4, we use the visible astrological model (World) to reflect back on the metaphysics. In this manner, we come to better understand both astrology and the metaphysical principles upon which it is based.

Between sections One and Being/Intelligence, Damiani inserts an "Interlude" on *qualitative* mathematics. In this, he shows how the fundamental meanings of numbers, one through 10, are "prefigured" in Plotinus' analysis of the "complexities" of the One. This exploration of the complexities of the One deals with critical issues underlying metaphysics, theology, and any other approach to the Ultimate. The numbers are also critical in determining the order and meaning of various astrological terms.

Of the four sections, the first is the only one that Damiani had finished before he died in 1984. The rest he left in various stages of incompletion. It took 16 years for his obviously brilliant and dedicated students to put this book together. It was necessary to augment what Damiani had completed of Astronoesis, per se, with some of his notes, lectures, and unpublished essays. This included work in astrology which employed the ideas of the theosophist, T. Subba Row. Consequently, many important meanings of astrological terms are carried by mostly Hindu and Buddhist terminology. Although Plotinus is included here, these sections don't have the elegance of the first.

Nevertheless, we are given plenty to go on. This is an intelligently and gorgeously executed book. It is rich with illuminating diagrams and fine explanatory essays. For those with an affinity for this kind of "rational mysticism" and/or astrology, this is truly a book of wisdom. It enhances both fields and will perhaps revolutionize our evaluation of astrology—if not, indeed our cosmos.

New Perspectives: Spring 2003, pp 53, 54

Getting to the Heart of Zen Teachings

Mud and Water: The Collected Teachings of Zen Master Bassui

Translated by Arthur Braverman

(Wisdom Publications; 256 pp.)

At Home in the Muddy Water: A Guide to Finding Peace Within Everyday Chaos

By Ezra Bayda

(Shambhala; 158 pp.)

Reviewed by Bill Gilbert

My first contact with Bassui was through the translations in Kapleau's *Three Pillars of Zen*. Braverman's revised translation will give the serious Zen student an even clearer picture of Bassui's practice.

Although Braverman presents an easy-to-read translation, the reader who does not know the original language should explore other translations as well. Here are two translations of the same first line from Bassui's lecture on One Mind.

a.) Kapleau: "If you would free yourself of the sufferings of the Six Realms, you must learn the direct way to become a Buddha. This way is no other than the realization of your own mind."

b.) Braverman: "If you want to avoid the suffering of life and death, you must know the way to Buddhahood this very moment. The way to Buddhahood is to realize your own mind."

Note that some parts are almost identical, but the reader may have to know special terms to understand other parts. Through two (or more) translations, the reader can come to a clearer picture of the original.

In his introduction, Braverman presents Bassui's most famous koan which he gave to his students at his death:

> Bassui sat erect in zazen posture, turned to his disciples, and said: 'Look directly! What is this? Look in this manner and you will not be fooled.' He repeated this injunction in a loud voice and died.

In part of his extensive introduction, Braverman writes much about the known Zen masters at the time of Bassui and asserts that Bassui's enlightenment was "verified" by Koho Kakumyo tracing the lineage of masters. However, he notes that Bassui "makes no mention of this connection—or any other for that matter."

Nevertheless, Braverman then proceeds to describe the lineage and the activities in Zen at that time, much that is interesting. However, the reader of the text should consider carefully what to do with this interpretive material. A Zen student can study and meditate on the translations of Bassui and gain greatly from them. A person who wants merely to see Bassui's works in a historical perspective may not gain as much.

This book is a valuable addition to any serious library on Zen. The key question for students of Zen who do not spend their lives in a monastery is how to develop a practice that fits into daily life. Ezra Bayda attempts to deal with this question in *At Home in the Muddy Water*.

His key idea is to "practice" to avoid an "artificial" or "substitute" life, one in which we are controlled by beliefs, usually based on fear or unfulfilled expectations. For one example, Bayda tells the reader to sit and concentrate on sensations in the body.

"If there is any discomfort, don't try to avoid it or change it. Instead, feel the quality of the experience." Sitting this way, according to Bayda will eventually reduce the power of the beliefs underlying such states—in this case the belief that you should be comfortable and can't be happy unless you are.

In the chapter, "Practicing with Sexuality," Bayda is more of a psychologist than a Zen teacher, dealing with problems people have with sexuality as mainly guilt and the problem of not talking about one's beliefs about sexuality.

This brings me to the main problem I have in following Bayda's ideas. How does one identify a belief? Pierre Grimes (in *Philosophical Midwifery...*) says a belief "assumes something about an actual state of affairs, without any knowledge to support its claim; yet one thinks, feels, and acts as if it represented the actual condition of some state of affairs."

Using this definition, beliefs may not be as obvious as Bayda claims. We hold beliefs as if they are knowledge; therefore, we will have to do something to see through this self-delusion. If one can't see clearly a belief one holds, getting rid of it is not guaranteed no matter how long one "practices."

New Perspectives: Winter 2004, p. 43

Reality

by Peter Kingsley
(Golden Sufi Center; 600 pp.)
Reviewed by Juan Balboa

During and after having read Professor Kingsley's new book, which he named "Reality," I felt much the same, I dare say, as Socrates felt about his own self-perception, versus that presented of him by his accusers; for in *The Apology*, which is Plato's account of Socrates' defense of the charges brought against him by three men who represented three groups of Athenian society, Socrates begins his defense by stating, "O men of Athens, how you, on the one hand, have been affected by my accusers, I do not know, but I, on the other hand, hardly recognized myself, since they spoke so persuasively." This sentiment, is what I felt towards the way I have grown to know Plato and to understand the philosophy that supernally flows through him versus the way that he has now been presented to us by Professor Kingsley. For Kingsley presents to us a picture of Plato as an unscrupulous and therefore unjust playwright of fictions that is not below taking the philosophy of his father, Parmenides, and by an act of literary patricide, murdered the very heart of his meaning/logos. Indeed, according to Kingsley, not only is Plato guilty of this, but "philosophers have worked their hardest for more than two thousand years to make his 'it' some kind of logical abstraction that exists somewhere else—on the other level of reality. And they are bound to want to play around a little with his words; fudge their meaning here and there; do some careful mistranslating."

Yet his most amazing contention, is that Gorgias the sophist (sophists being proven by Socrates to be among the most imbecile of creatures) by his fraud/vice/*apate*, was able to accomplish what the Truth/Virtue/*arete* of Plato was not; that is, to draw them, to the intuitive insight of the very nature of Reality!

One of Gorgias' disciples, Meno, who instead, of being brought into a certain cathartic state by Socrates' art of midwifery, which finally draws forth out of one, that pure state of soul-searching that precedes any insight, brings up various rationalizations as to why the search for Reality is a fruitless search. Socrates then reveals to Meno, one aspect of The Great Doctrine of "priests and priestesses who have paid careful attention (*memeleke*) to the things of their ministry" The Doctrine of Reminiscence, which soundly proves that even an uneducated slave boy, by being properly led, can overcome all of Meno's objections and realize the object of his search.

New Perspectives: Fall 2005, p. 45

Acknowledging Parts of the Psyche

Big Mind • Big Heart: Finding Your Way

by Zen Master Dennis Genpo Merzel

Big Mind Publishing; 192 pp., CD included

Reviewed by Julie Postel

It is not often that the book comes out after the movie, but Zen Master Dennis Genpo Merzel has released the book with a CD which works along with the DVD which was reviewed in the last issue of New Perspectives Journal. In "Big Mind/Big Heart: Finding Your Way" Genpo Merzel provides a way for us to recognize the parts of ourselves by calling them to the forefront of our thinking. Genpo Merzel uses his own voices to demonstrate the process as he integrates the different aspects into a whole after allowing them their individual expression. This reviewer recommends that the reader first experience track number one of the CD, then read the book, then watch the DVD and lastly listen to tracks 2 and 3 of the CD. In that order the material can be appreciated and used for a personal experience of the process which can assist the self-reflective person toward more awareness of their many "voices." This process is a way of making distinctions in the human psyche without ignoring the inherent paradox which arises when we see that all is one! For Genpo Merzel shows us that we can call on a specific voice to get in touch with its aspect, and while doing so, it is impossible not to be affected in the present moment.

In this most important time in our life on this planet, anything which can wake us up to deal with our present crises in a balanced and wholesome way is most welcome! As a philosopher, this reviewer wonders what can be accomplished if we do not go further than voicing our many parts, even if they become more integrated by this method. For if the reflective person does not continue past the recognition of states of mind and their functions to figuring out the source of our continuing imbalances on this planet, we may feel better and be happier, but when we are faced with great problems, we may not work to understand them. Genpo Merzel's method definitely appears to assist the participant in getting "unstuck" by shifting the attention from one voice to another, and this is a most excellent tool for mankind, especially when we try to see where someone else is coming from. Genpo Merzel offers his own voices as examples in his book, and it is very interesting to see the effect of speaking from a particular aspect; for example, as he expresses generosity, he becomes generous as he writes from that voice. Also, it is interesting to see that many of the voices know about one another and can speak about the Self or the Non-Grasping Mind or Big Mind or Big Heart from their perspective. In that way, the process maintains a healthy integration and does not ask the person to completely split off from themselves while concentrating on one or another aspect of themselves.

As we use this material it becomes interesting to note when the voices are speaking in the third person and when they speak in the first person, for those shifts in perspective make it clear that we don't need to allow states of mind such as *fear* to take over as the speaker for the whole self while giving voice to our fears without holding back. If world leaders could gather together and engage in this process, it would serve as a good beginning for creating the space where understanding can begin.

Julie Postel (formerly Grabel) recently married, is a student of philosophy, and is owner of Opening Mind Associates in support of the Noetic Society, Inc. She also owns a small bar code label business and loves to dance.

New Perspectives: Winter 2008, p. 43

Philosopher Contrasts Beliefs with Understanding

Is It All Relative?

By Pierre Grimes

(Hyparxis; 134 pp.)

Editor's review by Bill Gilbert

This book begins with a play, a dialogue that switches between the main characters—Joseph, Harry, and Elea—talking in a coffee shop. They are discussing a common phrase and its variations commonly heard both now and in the past and the reasoning behind it—"it's all relative," "there is no view better than any other," "it's all interpretation, man is the measure." These are heard daily in discourse, and too few of us challenge them and the people who say them. This play puts forth that challenge.

The jewel of the book after the play is the section on analogy, which explores (as probably nowhere else) most completely how to use analogies, similes, and metaphors. Joseph says, "When men use allegories, similes, analogies to find natural parallels with their experiences, they not only become more rational but also preserve their roles in society, and they keep alive their traditions." He asks, "Does this kind of inquiry interest you?" (p.45) Many relegate analogy to a small role in reasoning because one cannot "prove" something with an analogy; however, the goal of self-knowledge is to *understand.* Analogies are uniquely suited for this.

Joseph shows how important and challenging to life *understanding* is as contrasted with *believing.* He reports the challenge of Sophronicus, a friend of the owner of the café: "The quest for understanding the Self ... surfaces a distrust of the process... because it awakens the dreaded sense of the unknown and brings us face to face with the fear of losing control since none of us welcomes fundamental changes in our lives." (p.93)

We have become so *knowing* in our modern world—even sometimes thinking it is better to pretend we know (even to ourselves) than to admit we don't know and seek the truth. Read this book not for answers but for questions and wonder.

Are there negative aspects to the book? Yes. You will not get what the book has to offer by simply sitting down and reading it one more time. As I have done, you will read this book over and over again and find something new in it each time.

Independent Review by Nobuya Teraoka

To enter into the challenge given in this book is to enter into the Platonic challenge: to uncover, examine, and understand the false beliefs that block one from the nature of Reality. Just as the characters in *Is It All Relative?* actively question and answer each other and thereby reach personally meaningful insights about themselves and the puzzling nature of Reality, so also, by actively engaging this book in a similar way, the reader will come face to face with the hollowness of his most cherished beliefs, learned both in his family and in society, and realize the heavy cost of holding such beliefs. For just as the character Harry cannot explore a question and follow the implications of his response until he has been forced to see that he is ignorant of his ignorance, so also the reader will not be able to follow the questions raised and explored in this book unless he realizes that he has not yet learned to read and listen without interpreting.

Indeed the nature and power of interpretation is the main issue of this book and the book's true significance is its power to break through interpretation. Because the book raises and investigates the problem of interpretation by means of dialogue, just as Plato does in his dialogues like the *Theaetetus*, the reader can explore his own difficulties by studying the difficulties the characters themselves face. Further, like Plato, Pierre Grimes uses analogy to explore interpretation and has included in the appendix a very fine study of the importance of analogy in philosophy. Once one understands the nature and power of interpretation, then one can begin to uncover what specific false beliefs hinder one from entering into a pure state of wonder in which true Being resplendently shines.

Bill Gilbert is Lecturer Emeritus at California State University in Long Beach, California. He is publisher and editor of Hyparxis Press. Nobuya Teraoka is a philosopher at Golden West College in Huntington Beach, California. He also teaches mathematics.

New Perspectives: Winter 2008, p. 46

Section Six: THEMES

State of Consciousness

Turning it Around

By Pierre Grimes

Guest Editor, Theme Section

We have been told our condition. It may well be that we face a terrible fate—the extinction of human life on our planet. We have been warned enough, and we know only too well the predictions.

We can look for answers from religion, from our educational institutions or the State, and from those who make it their business to study future trends.

Many religious people see the collapse and ruination of the planet as having been foretold by their faith, and actions to reverse it would deny their faith. But should some of the faithful survive long enough to watch the final collapse, believing their own faith is being confirmed, they can at least wonder why our ignorance was the instrument of a divine will.

Our educational institutions do the bidding of the State, and before educational institutions can confirm something happening, it must already have reached such an advanced stage of decay that the planet would have reached its terminal condition.

Can this thing we call the State help us understand and deal with this crisis? Any review of the record of the modern State would show it has been the principle player in this disaster. Consider, have we not witnessed two world wars and a vicious cold war that spawned local wars that destroyed millions of people? In our century more people have been murdered by their own governments in times of peace then those killed in wars between states. Is this but madness and unleashed ignorance? The modern state is sovereign and that sovereignty means it must advance its own will or destiny at the expense of other states. The needs of the whole are lost in its drive to satisfy the needs of some part of itself, so it cannot deal with the fact that its own unjust policies are bringing the earth to the crisis of its existence.

Looking back on this century, we can see that it was not madness and ignorance that drove this machine of the state. It was an idealism that offered itself as the standard of justice. While many contributed to this unholy vision, we know that Hegel, Marx, Nietzsche, and Freud were regarded as its visionaries. The dream of the nineteenth century thinkers became the nightmare of the twentieth century. Perhaps, we should wonder about what new dream is being fashioned for this next century.

If there are those who can honestly face our past and present and still have the courage to look into the future, we should listen to them. If they can give us any sign of hope, we should invite them to share their vision with us. We have heard enough of the tales of woe and despair and we don't need any more proselytizing apocalyptic scenarios because deep inside we know we have to find a way to save ourselves and the planet. But I think we know something else. We know if we succeed, we will have become better ourselves in the act of saving ourselves.

The numerous seers today have visions which are so different from those earlier nineteenth century dreamers that a quantum jump separates the one from the other. These contemporary thinkers can describe the transformative forces underlying man's spiritual evolution because they themselves have participated in that very process. They speak from their own experience and extrapolate their experience into a vision of the future. These men include Sri Aurobindo, Pierre Teilhard de Chardin, Peter D. Ouspensky, Aldous Huxley, and Peter Russell. Each of these men has offered a solution to man's condition. The theme is evolution, the evolution of mankind. But biological evolution takes a long period of time to bring about changes, and that is something we don't have. It is not that some individuals won't continue to reach their full spiritual potential, but that man as a whole must evolve, each and every one of us, and all at once. The idea of a global and species wide development, as with Chardin, relieves the individual from having to play a significant part in his/her own transformation. Could the changes be taking place all around us, so we could see the new Adam emerging about us? It will be easy to see because its noble appearance wouldn't be part of the contemporary forms of our present age, such as nihilism. You might ask, how might the new Adam come into existence?

Well, for one thing there are spiritual methods and techniques, such as prayer, meditation, and the whole range of spiritual forms of yoga that might become the means for the new Adam to emerge. If any work, it would have to be applied on a large scale to reverse the degeneration that is currently taking place. Maybe hope exists because today many people reach each other through our electronic Internet communicating devices and through them to teach these methods to all. Through the competition of one spiritual system with another, a superior form may emerge. Peter Russell advances this possibility and argues strongly for its adoption.

Peter Russell's new book, *The Global Brain Awakens*, does that very thing since he brings together the insights of the physical and social sciences, modern technological advances, and the mystical traditions into a splendid unity that effectively argues that mankind will survive only through enlightenment. Russell appeals to a variety of evidence to show that mankind will meet the next challenge and successfully emerge into the next phase of the evolution of consciousness as enlightened roshis, saints, and Buddhas. He points to the fact that the number of people involved in the consciousness movement has been doubling about every five years, both the number of individuals and organizations. When any continuous doubling phenomena occur such that the rate of increase is directly proportional to its current size, it can be described as a natural growth process. Thus, the degree to which numbers attracted to this cause are drawn from those "success achievers," "traditional value people" and others, leads Russell to believe that a natural growth process powers the new consciousness age. If the growth process continues it will surpass in numbers and importance of those in the present Information Age.

Russell draws the reader to see a new age giving birth to a new class of teachers and heroes, a new set of ideals, and a new way of relating to one another. To meet this need Russell sees the need for a new class of spiritual teachers who will not only be the communicators of wisdom, but directly pass on such wisdom to others.

New Perspectives: August/September 1996, pp. 44, 45

Living/Dying/Death

Living and Dying with Zen

By Barbara Stecker

Philip Kapleau is well known as the author of the classic *Three Pillars of Zen.* Indeed, that book is a very difficult act to follow since it includes interviews with Yasutani Roshi, one of the foremost Zen roshis of the 20th century, the 14th century writings of Bassui, peerless among Zen seekers, and several accounts from those who achieved kensho, so that we may also see what modern Zen practice is like, not to mention what kensho does and doesn't do for the sitter's life.

The Zen of Living and Dying (revised and reedited in 1998) is a match for this work on the level of thoroughness and expertise. There are writings on every aspect of dying, death, funerals, living wills, the bereaved, and more. Kapleau has again taken the approach of including many voices and many thinkers who present intellectual, emotional, spiritual, and physical accounts of dying and death. The array of material would permit one to individualize one's own dying experience and death or ameliorate the passage of a loved one. On the highest level, his goal is to present an art of dying.

> "To die artfully is to die thinking of nothing, wishing for nothing, wanting to understand nothing, clinging to nothing—just fading away like the clouds in the sky. That is the acme of artful dying; such an accomplishment, though, presupposes considerable spiritual insight."

Indeed, it would appear to be an achievement quite on the level of Maha Samadhi, although I think that "fading away" is a poetic image rather than an accurate account since the soul doesn't fade or become less in the moments leading up to death: fading is what the physical being goes through.

While I have some Buddhist experience—Zen Buddhism with Yasutani Roshi and Maezumi Roshi at UCLA, Theravada Buddhism with Shingen Young, Korean Buddhism with Myo Bong S'nim and Pierre Grimes at the Opening Mind Academy, and Tibetan Buddhist visualizations—I am finally a Platonist and a student of Grimes' Dialectic.

As a Platonist, I practice a philosopher's yoga—from Plato's *Phaedo*: "The fact is, those who tackle philosophy aright are simply and solely practicing dying, practicing death, all the time, but nobody sees it." As you can see from this quote, a philosopher worthy of the name is always practicing dying and death.

One such philosophical practice of dying from the *Phaedo* is purification—"And is not purification really that which has been mentioned so often in our discussion, to separate as far as possible the soul from the body, and to accustom it to collect itself together out of the body in every part, and to dwell alone by itself as far as it can, both at this present and in the future, being freed from the body as if from a prison?"

This collection and separation is for the sake of wisdom:

> "And I suppose it reasons best when none of these senses disturbs it, hearing or sight, or pain, or pleasure indeed, but when it is completely by itself and says good-bye to the body, and so far as possible has no dealings with it, when it reaches out and grasps that which really is… And is it not then that the philosopher's soul chiefly holds the body cheap and escapes from it, while it seeks to be by itself?"

In this state of separation the philosopher's soul reaches what *is*, the nature of reality.

New Perspectives: Winter 2004, pp. 54, 55

Dream Your Life

Learn While Dreaming Your Life

Pierre Grimes

Guest editor for "Dream Your Life" theme for our next issue.

When I was enjoying a drink at our local pub, listening to the usual talk, there came a lull in our talk and at that time a foreign-looking gentleman joined us and so friendly he was that it seemed as if we had known him for years. Once settled, he offered to share a tale with us, and we agreed to listen. The tale he spun forth was like those grand Russian Mirrors that reflect one another, creating levels of reality as far as you can see. I find this story intrudes itself upon me at the worst of times. I would prefer to ignore it and say it's only a story so I thought maybe by sharing it I could stop wondering about it.

I will try to recall his story as best as I am able, but I am aware that I won't be able to express it the way he told it:

> "Well," he said, "There was once a remarkable mask and costume musical party that I attended that was hosted by Gabriel de la Phillippo, the famous magician-artist, at his home in Amsterdam. To my surprise I soon discovered that not one of the beautifully costumed guests could say who had invited them. Equally, none could describe how they arrived at the party. However, it was clear that this kind of failure didn't disturb the guests since it didn't interfere with what any of them were doing. The gaiety of the party was so absorbing that when anyone left the party they tacitly agreed among themselves not to discuss where the person was going nor inquire why they had to leave when they did.
>
> "As curious as I found this to be what was far more curious, if not mystifying, was that all of the guests were acting out the role that was consistent with the mask and costume they wore. I noticed something very strange about the masks because the masks could go

through a wide range of changes while remaining the same mask. It took awhile before I realized that changes to the mask were consistent with the variations in the role they played so that the many turns and twists in the role brought forth corresponding changes in the mask.

"Further, during the party I saw that the games they played brought the guests to both tears and laughter but for all that only a few came to see the need to entirely switch their mask and costume for another and these few did it in the same way. As they peeled off the old mask a new one beneath the old one appeared and as they took off their costume another underneath took the place of the old.

"What I found most strange and disturbing about these changes was that the design for the new costume and mask reflected precisely whoever and whatever convinced them that the old mask and costume had fit them. As for the guests, each continued to dance and play without missing a single step since they experienced no difficulty adjusting to the new turns and twists in their mask and their changing costumes.

"Madness is what I saw and it seemed to me that the chaos of appearance was set upon another appearance so that the irrational seemed to be reigning supreme. I had seen enough so I diligently sought out our host, Gabriel de la Phillippo, for an explanation of this strange party.

"After some difficulty I found him by the bar and after I explained to him what I thought of his mad party he merely smiled and gave me a card. However, it was too dark for me to read it at the time so I carefully put it in my pocket so that I might read it afterwards.

"Later, I found the proper place to read it and it said, 'Each of my guests finds their own way here to play out the lives they have been persuaded to play and until they learn that no mask and costume can fit the astonishing beauty of the nature of the Self they will continue to live a dream they need not play.'

"Say our life is like a dream if you like and go on and say a tale is another dream but tell me who has wakened from the dream we call our life?"

Our storyteller finished. Gather this together and ask, "Who is the craftsman of these dreams and tales and can there be a life that is awake and not a dream?"

New Perspectives: Winter 2004, p. 2

Dream Your Life

Understanding Ourselves Through Dreams

We have the wisdom of the ages available. With the use of this knowledge and some direction we can learn about ourselves by the study of our dreams.

By Pierre Grimes

Guest Editor, Dream Section

We are the inheritors of several ancient traditions, and while each of them has contributed to our present they are not all accepted by most of us nor equally honored. The practical Roman influence, and the piety of Judaic-Christian influence are well known and accepted, but we have not come to terms with the ancient Greek culture as we should. We have understood the Greeks through the eyes of Christians and only saw pagan thought. Through the practical eyes of the Romans we only saw the beginnings of science and mathematics. Slowly, thoughtfully, and cautiously, some of our clearest thinkers have announced that when we allow Greek thought to be seen for what it is in its own terms and in its highest vision, we see a spiritual tradition that can rival the claims of the Judaic-Christian-Islamic religions. We can see this most clearly in the study of dreams, since dreams are oracles, and from them man can gain a spiritual direction independent of these belief based religions.

Freud opened the door to the study of dreams in Europe, and it was accepted because it was used as a tool to uncover human pathology. Jung extended it, but was cautious, claiming all dreams were a projection of the dynamics of the self. Plato was among the ancient Greeks who claimed that dreams could lead us to truth and to the knowledge of the present, past, and future. Thus, in seeking help from dreams we are returning to a Hellenic world that we can approach either in a practical or spiritual way. The number of books that have been published recently reflect these approaches: the practical do it yourself books, such as Joan Mazza's *Dream Back Your Life*, the healing approach used by Marc Ian Barasch in his *Healing Dreams*, that moves from psychology cautiously to the spiritual; and the work of Edward Tick that brings Ancient Greek mysteries into modern medicine with *The Practice of Dream Healing*.

The idea of healing has for many of us the image of recovering from physical ills and that is too restrictive and narrow. The Hellenics called the healer the one who can see what others ignore, who can use incantations, who has mastered breath control to gain awareness beyond our everyday experience, and especially to learn through dreams what contributes to the illness. Iatromantis was a prophetic physician, and is another name for the God Apollo and is applied to those in his healing tradition. Peter Kingsley's *In The Dark Places of Wisdom* explores these themes and links them to Parmenides, the father of philosophy.

It is our age alone that has been gifted with the wisdom of the ages; we are the people who have available to us the works of all spiritual and religious traditions. Teachers from many lands are here to share their wisdom with us. What before was hidden or simply not accessible is in our lap and we can now reach out and enter into it. What we need is direction, confidence in ourselves, and the assurance that our journey is not in vain. However, it is not at all easy to determine if we have applied correctly what we have been learning or if we have missed something important in our studies. Teachers may or may not give satisfying answers to these questions and that leaves us wondering if we just might learn the answers from ourselves. Dreams do this very thing. We all know that it is not an easy task to understand dreams and that is their curious gift. For the understanding of dreams is never literal; it always reflects images from our present and past which are expressed symbolically, and are associated with the problems we are working on. The understanding of dreams forces us to use our minds in a way that is referred to as functional understanding, which is their gift. This is a new way to understand not only ourselves but others as well. Another gift we gain by this study is the realization that there must be something that crafts our dreams, that is aware of our present and of our past difficulties,of the spiritual direction we are currently taking; and that has our best interest at heart. Symbolically it represents all this to help us understand ourselves in a perfectly performed narrative play that we call our dream.

I call it the Master Craftsman of our Dreams, and since it works for our personal benefit it is best to say that for all who dream, it extends itself throughout the universe providing to all who dream a gift of goodness.

New Perspectives: Winter 2005, p. 34

Dream Your Life

Dreams, Fantasies, and Daydreams

A journal from a recent five day Esalen Dream Workshop with Pierre Grimes, Ph.D.

By Julie Grabel

Monday

Esalen has already begun her transformation because Pierre Grimes is here and has already worked the group into the same high level of functioning which is usual by the last day, but rare on the first! This is summer Esalen number twelve, I think. The catalogue description has prepared us to explore our dreams, daydreams and fantasies for five days. Those of us who have been studying with Dr. Grimes join him here to see ourselves and push ourselves to learn his Art, a rational method for understanding. Newcomers are quickly brought into the process, and Dr. Grimes provides the guidance so that no one is left out.

Dr. Grimes has already done one person's dream, and that person is astounded by the profound simplicity. Her dream was short which just made it easier for Dr. Grimes to guide her to the insights available through exploring her dream methodically. She and her husband are surprised and thrilled by the level of intelligibility and the non-interpretive aspects of Philosophical Midwifery (Grimes' methodology). Dr. Grimes has also explored what I would call a waking dream, but it was also a realization. It has taken me a long time to see that he uses the same method to explore whatever is offered because he can vary the questioning for each person.

When a dream is recorded as soon as possible and then transcribed we gain the clearest picture of the original dream, but even an older dream which has only been recollected out loud can be understood to some degree. First we divide the dream into its natural divisions, as if the dream were a movie and you are dividing it into scenes. Then each scene is studied for its words, its activity, and the states of mind which are present in the dream. Then a certain amount of questioning and pondering brings us to see the dream as a story with some sort of a goal, and we see if the goal is met and if not, when and what happened. If met, was the goal maintained? Where is the problem in the dream itself? What state of mind is present during the problem? By this time in an exploration the dreamer has usually recognized the state of mind and can begin to see the role that state of mind has in the daily life, but I get ahead of myself.

Reflecting on a dialogue with some people in the hot tubs earlier in the day, someone asked me about our workshop, and I said, "We are seeing that our dreams are intelligible and that they are for our benefit. If explored, we can benefit further by seeing the condition of our mind right now. Our dreams show us something we have ignored or something we have overlooked and while we are exploring these dreams, we are also learning about the creator of our dreams. We conclude that it is *one* since it can be seen so clearly that whatever generates the dream is not only aware of the dreamer's past, present and future, but also everyone else's too and the Dream Master (Dr. Grimes' name for this providential Being) uses it all "to craft the perfect multimedia event for the dreamer" in order to have maximum potential for benefit. I also said that by exploring our dreams we can move from a fated existence to one gifted with Providence.

Monday afternoon's session had us counting from one to ten over and over again! It's an exercise Dr. Grimes has used many times to assist us in seeing spontaneous daydreams which occur when you set your mind to a task and see what pops in to interrupt. We're looking to understand the moment we enter into the daydream and the moment we wake up from it. The exercise is to watch or hear the numbers one through ten and ask yourself, "Where do they come from, where do they go?" By instructing the mind to engage in this one-pointed task, we see what happens to interrupt it—and whatever it is that interrupts turns out to be based on an image of the self. Implicit in that image is a view of oneself, a belief which even carries over to a belief about the nature of Reality. We explored one participant's spontaneous daydream, and it is interesting that the daydream and attendant state of mind took the participant back to past scenes where he saw the image of his daydream take its shape. The model for learning provided by his parents has been picked up, and he uses it now even though it doesn't help, but rather hinders him from reaching his goals. Dr. Grimes says that understanding will not happen from the present examples of the state of mind but will be possible from the past learning scene since that is the model that was being used unreflectively until now. (Why that is true can be seen in his book.)

I am fascinated by the intelligibility of my experiences—that the spontaneous daydream experiences are bringing in the same themes I have seen in previous midwifery talks—memory and stupidity. Dr. Grimes also gives a guided meditation to start us off in a daydream: he presents the beginning of a story and we complete it. It reveals a lot about our individual views of the world to complete the story and several of us read our written daydream out loud, and we see this type of daydream is different from the spontaneous one—the state of mind is not as clear, it's more subtle, but a good listener can spot it.

We then get to explore the first dream which was dreamed while at this Esalen workshop and a lot of us are sleepy, ready for dreams of our own. One participant gained an insight into a state of mind from his dream that he saw in his waking world, but when Dr. Grimes finished bringing out the dream's dynamics and it was obvious that the man had experienced that state in his recent life, Dr. Grimes could tell that the man was not open to exploring the personal aspects any further and so he said, "You see where it goes?" to which the man said, "Yes." And the session was over.

Tuesday

Last night's hot tub discussion took a beginner into the reflective way of thinking about our families and Dr. Grimes suggested that a play could be written to show in three acts the conditions, the onset and the conclusion of a personal pathologos or sick belief. Using the transgenerational model, we see the dharma being passed, grandparent to parent to child—same state of mind, same result. The newcomer saw it for herself in her own life. Two other dreamers are taken through explorations and both are filled with insights once they do the work of structuring the dreams, adding states of mind, seeing the logos (the words, the language) and then dealing with the activity in terms of a drama.

For the first time, Dr. Grimes introduced the Esalen workshop to the Dream Master as a new divinity! He brought us to see that the Dream Master functions in a way which subsumes all other divinity, so it may not be a god! The *One* is above the Dream Master, but not much else is! For it is awake to everything—past, present and future and seeks our benefit in presenting us with a picture of our mind.

Dr. Grimes tells us to ask the Dream Master to let us be awake in our dreams, to see the degree of freedom we can have to direct the dream. So, after going to the hot tubs and listening to the dialogue between Dr. Grimes and one of the newcomers to his method about spiritual systems and enlightenment, I slept like a baby and didn't have any dreams.

Wednesday

Dr. Grimes is on fire with ideas about the Dream Master and is cultivating group mind with his questions about naming and function. If something has the proper name, it reflects its function appropriately. If the Dream Master functions to provide material for our benefit continuously and at all times considering where a person is at and what level of development the person is in, what is needed in order to grow, what will benefit right now—what name? It does more than provide our dreams—it loves us properly! It may be the perfect parent.

A reporter from the Los Angeles Times is visiting our session, and I can tell Dr. Grimes is directing his exploration at not only assisting the dreamer, but also giving enough of the structure of his method so that she can follow along. It's amazing how effortlessly he incorporates comments about the progress of the exploration and because the person who is exploring the dream is an experienced pregnant party (the term for the person exploring a dream, a daydream or a personal problem and the person assisting is called the midwife), he is able to move along very quickly into recognizing the state of mind which the dream is pointing out. He was able to make connections into the past which brought a deep level of insight. It is during this exploration that we see most clearly that the solution is not in the present, but is in the past. By going back into the past, the person is able to see the drama played out, see the states of mind and figure out what was really happening in the scene, what the functions of each person were and then the proper name is applied to that functioning—for example, when someone sees that what they had always thought was an act of justice in the past scene actually turns out to function as sabotage, they might put the name of traitor on the person in the scene and then by using that name in the present gain an insight into their own behavior.

Two dreams are explored in the kitchen in between formal sessions! No stopping for this workshop leader—almost continually exploring something with someone, sitting in the meditation hall or sleeping a few hours. Amazing vitality.

Thursday

I missed the hot tub discussion last night because I went to sleep. But it was fun getting recollections at breakfast and beyond—about how to use part, whole, unity, union, communion, and oneness in terms of dream work. When the dreamer is seeing and having insights about past, present and possibly future times, the dreamer is in union with the dream. When the whole group is sharing in the insights at the same time, there is communion.

The whole talk on these principles which was extended into the workshop session is very worth listening to. One of our participants had the Esalen group dream (we have learned that during such an intense set of explorations, one person will have a dream which pertains to us all) and it was explored. The dream was simple and in four parts and pointed to her opportunity for a gift which she would need to move toward to accept rather than having it handed to her.

My own personal exploration was tonight and it came out of the image from Tuesday which I finally revealed at the end of this evening. With Dr. Grimes' mastery I recollected a state of mind of being neglected and mistreated which in my childhood, was followed by my leaving the house for long periods of time. We explored the general milieu (regular daily, around-the-house everyday way of being) with my mother, and I discovered that I had come to a wordless conclusion. I never put it into words so it wasn't available to be reflected upon. I thought she had a desire to get rid of me because I was stupid—but upon fair examination, it turned out to be a desire to get rid of me so that she could read and drink and smoke without interruption! I remembered that I did a lot of wandering as a child in order to get away from the yelling and anger. When we studied the way that anger functions, I saw why my mother wanted to get me to leave her alone. Understanding takes place when we compare the way a person was functioning in a past scene with the milieu. As we make sense of what happens and the reasons for our behavior, I am surprised at how obvious it is. But that is part of the puzzle—to discover why we believe our parents at these times. And as we practice this way of seeing, the quality of life broadens and deepens with excellence whenever one gains an insight in this way.

Before my exploration, I had missed a talk about Providence which was indeed showering me with goodness all through the week! What is the Dream Master? Is it Providence? Is it Oneness? Is it the first Oneness? Is it prior to Rest, Motion, Same, Different and Being (the five first principles in Platonic metaphysics)? Discussions on the dialectic and naming fill the air.

Friday

Dr. Grimes explores a fantasy that comes up for one of the participants while he is meditating. His state of mind was anger, and he saw it as a tangent because in order to advance in meditation he would need to stay in silence. But that silence conflicted with his model of love and learning from his past which had angry outbursts. Again we have themes of anger and love.

Then we explore a dream fragment—having already explored dreams, daydreams (two kinds), random thoughts, fantasies, and personal problems. This particular fragment is rich in logos which is contradictory or puzzling, indicating that there is a false conclusion afoot! The participant sees how scary it is to challenge the old belief and how scary it was to challenge the authority in the past—we cannot without feeling exiled as children, but we have the opportunity to do so as adults.

Esalen ends on a very high note—the Dream Master and Pierre Grimes—what a pair! Thank you. While dream work done in this way is perhaps the most accessible route to seeing the conditions of one's mind, the states of mind which are revealed in this work can serve as the springboard to further explorations in order to discover the source of our beliefs and to uncover the reasons why we believe what we believe. There is no doubt that our dreams are gifts which benefit us and they can be opened in varying degrees depending on the dreamer's courage and how fully the dream is explored.

New Perspectives: Winter 2005, pp. 35, 36, 42

Dream Your Life

The Prophetic Dream

By Juan Balboa

Three days before our beloved hero, Socrates, was put to death by the Athenian democracy, he had a prophetic dream, minutes before he awoke on his own, to find his lifelong friend watching him sleep. Socrates then enquires of his friend why he did not wake him, to which he answers that he did not want to wake him since he was sleeping so peacefully. Socrates then relates to his friend that it was providential that he did not wake him since he had just received a prophetic dream. Now, concerning dreams of this kind, Iamblichus, one of the last successors to Plato's Academy, relates to us this beautiful and concise passage:

> "But the dreams which are denominated *theopemptoi*, or sent from God, do not subsist after the manner you mention; but they take place either when sleep is leaving us, and we are beginning to awake, and then we hear a certain voice, which concisely tells us

what is to be done; or voices are heard by us, between sleeping and waking, or when we are perfectly awake."

The reception of these types of dreams was held in high regard by many ancient Hellenic mystics, starting from Orpheus, and including such figures as Pythagorus, Socrates, Plato, and Parmenides, as Professor Kingsley has recently brought to light in his book, *The Dark Places of Wisdom*.

Professor Grimes, whose articles appear in this magazine, is, in our own day, a spiritual man, as described by Socrates in The Symposium. He is also a master in dream works, following not only the ancient tradition, but also that of modern psychiatrists like Carl Jung.

The following "Hymn of Orpheus" is quite ancient, and it shows the reverence in which The Dream Master was held.

(85) To the Divinity of Dreams (Ονειροι)
The Fumigation from Aromatics

Thee I invoke, blest pow'r of dreams divine,
Angel of future fates, swift wings are thine:
Great source of oracles to human kind,
When stealing soft, and whisp'ring to the mind,
Thro' sleep's sweet silence, and the gloom of Night,
Thy pow'r awakes th' intellectual fight;
To silent souls the will of heaven relates,
And silently reveals their future fates,
Forever friendly to the upright mind,
Sacred and pure, to holy rites inclin'd;
For these with pleasing hope thy dreams inspire,
Bliss to anticipate, which all desire.
Thy visions manifest of fate disclose,
What methods best may mitigate our woes;
Reveal what rites the Gods immortal please,
And what the means their anger to appease:
Forever tranquil is the good man's end,
Whose life, thy dreams admonish and defend.
But from the wicked turn'd averse to bless,
Thy form unseen, the angel of distress;
No means to check approaching ill they find,
Pensive with fears, and to the future blind.
Come, blessed pow'r, the signatures reveal

Which Heav'n's decrees mysteriously conceal,
Signs only present to the worthy mind,
Nor omens ill disclose of monstrous kind.

References in the introduction and the poem itself are from "Iamblichus on the Mysteries and the Life of Pythagorus," translated by Thomas Taylor (The Prometheus Trust). Juan Balboa is a long time student of Pierre Grimes and a member of the Opening Mind Academy in Costa Mesa, California. Balboa resides in San Jacinto, California..

New Perspectives: Winter 2005, pp. 39 & 41

A Special Report

Updating Work with Philosophical Midwifery:

We have pushed beyond our original boundary of exploration to include daydreams.

By Pierre Grimes, Ph.D.

The work I have engaged in over these years has been centered on exploring the reach of the mind. During that time it has become obvious that the acceptance of false beliefs about oneself is the very thing that blocks the effort to reach and understand the nature of the mind. As a consequence I have been exploring the difficulties and blocks that are experienced as one strives with excellence to realize one's personally meaningful goals, for since these false beliefs about oneself are unsuspected they only become visible when one struggles to achieve these goals. Once visible it is possible to understand why these false beliefs were believed to be true. When the conditions that made them believable are exposed, they drop away like autumn leaves.

In applying our method of Philosophical Midwifery to dreams we found it also possible to bring forward very positive ideas about one's existence. Probing the dream material we found that it is not unusual to bring out of the dreamer's forgetfulness more positive dimensions of their own dreams. Indeed, we have found that by the process of questioning some dreamers could recall forgotten episodes that were of major significance to them.

Among these positive dimensions we also found that enlightenment experiences—earlier experienced but forgotten by the dreamer—were recalled with all of their original vividness during the actual exploration. Thus, they benefited in three ways for they gained insights into the recalled dream, they recovered major meaningful spiritual experiences that they had forgotten, and they relived the recollections of those enlightenment dreams during the analysis itself.

We also have pushed beyond our original boundary of exploration to include daydreams. When subjects' daydreams were discussed and explored they found the initial image of themselves that they had identified with was one they had accepted as something essential to themselves. They saw that implicit in the image they had of themselves was a story that unfolded in the daydream. To see all the consequences of their self-image play out in their imagination—all the turns and twists, all the pain and suffering, all the victories and the defeats—left them with the sense of the futility of the daydream. However, when they began to realize that the self-image in their dream life was playing itself out in their daydreams they were able to see the connection between the two, daydreams and dreams.

In general then, our work continues to show that the mind constantly is communicating with us for our own benefit.

Each was a communication from their own mind, each offered them an opportunity to see their present situation in their dreams and the possibility that they may play out their daydreams in their everyday world. Surely, they saw that we often play out aspects of our daydreams, imitating in life what was played out in a daydream. Further, we offered our subjects an opportunity to see if even what might be called a random thought occurs when it does for a good reason and that it is itself a message worth pondering. In general then, our work continues to show that the mind constantly is communicating with us for our own benefit. The dream and daydream explorations were conducted during workshops; much of our work has been digitally recorded and is available on DVD's through our website.

Is it not true that when you know what to look for you often discover what you may not have expected to find? Thus, when we reread Homer's *Iliad* we were able to clearly discern the depth of Homer's understanding of human nature and how well he grasped the essential struggles man goes through to reach excellence with integrity. The results of this reflection became a series of articles posted in professional journals of philosophy dealing with Philosophical Midwifery in Homer's *Iliad.* It is in the same spirit that research into Plato brought us to see the depth of insight into his

Republic, because there he spelled out the need to study dreams with the aid of the logos and the law of the mind. Equally, we could say the same about reading Plato's *Parmenides* and Proclus' *Theology of Plato*, but that is another story. So, in conclusion, we are uncovering what had been lost of our profoundly deep heritage, we are finding a way to uncover it, to validate it in our everyday experience, and now we are pushing beyond those boundaries. In this process we are rediscovering a true spiritual philosophy, one that strives to understand the reach of the mind.

New Perspectives: Winter 2009, p.31.

Index

A

B

C

D

E

Y

Z

www.ingramcontent.com/pod-product-compliance
Ingram Content Group UK Ltd.
Pitfield, Milton Keynes, MK11 3LW, UK
UKHW041937190726
13854UKWH00004B/1633